*A Guide for
Advisors to Business Owners*

THE EXIT PLANNING COACH™ HANDBOOK

ALSO BY JOHN F. DINI

11 Things You Absolutely Need
to Know About Selling Your Business

Beating the Boomer Bust

Hunting in a Farmer's World:
Celebrating the Mind of an Entrepreneur

Your Exit Map: Navigating the Boomer Bust

*A Guide for
Advisors to Business Owners*

THE EXIT PLANNING COACH™ HANDBOOK

John F. Dini, CExP, CEPA

Gardendale Press

Copyright © 2022 by John F. Dini.
Published by Gardendale Press
15600 San Pedro Avenue Suite 200
San Antonio, TX 78232

All Rights Reserved. No part of this book may be used or reproduced by any means, graphic, electronic, or mechanical, including photocopying, recording, taping or by any information storage retrieval system without the express written permission of the author and publisher except in the case of brief quotations embodied in critical articles and reviews.

Because of the dynamic nature of the Internet, any Web addresses or links contained in this book may have changed since publication and may no longer be valid. The views expressed in this work are solely those of the author and do not necessarily reflect the views of the publisher.

Printed in the United States of America

Library of Congress Control Number: 2022921243

ISBN-10: 0-9790531-7-X
ISBN-13: 978-0-9790531-7-7

First Printing: December 2022
10 9 8 7 6 5 4 3 2 1

To Leila, my best friend,
my only love, and my partner in everything.

ACKNOWLEDGEMENTS

I want to express my appreciation to the hundreds of business owners and scores of professional advisors whose knowledge and wisdom were only summarized by me on these pages.

Thanks, as always, to our incredible team. Christi Brendlinger and Sarah Salgado have now worked on three books with me, not to mention innumerable articles, web content and blogs that they consistently make better.

Finally, my heartfelt gratitude to Rollo Tomassi and Keyser Söze, who remind me that not everything is as obvious as it might seem.

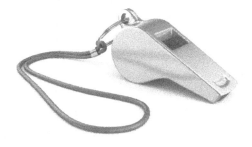

THE EXIT PLANNING COACH HANDBOOK
A Guide for Advisors to Business Owners

CONTENTS:

FORWARD:
We are on a Mission xvi

INTRODUCTION:
One professional to another.. xx

PART ONE: COACHING DISCOVERY
The Process..1

1. Coaching Before Advising 5
   Feeling The Rush...5
   The Advisory Rush 6
   To a Hammer..7
   What is Coaching Skill?...9
   The Most Important Question 10

2. Why Coaching Owners is Different..13
   The Buck Stops Here 13
   It's My Money 14
   It's My Baby...15
   It's My Decision 16

3. "I am Not a Coach!"..19

4. "My Clients Hate the Word Exit." 23

5. "I Don't need a Coach"..27

6. Lifestyle or Legacy? 31
   What Kind of Owner are You Coaching? 31
   What is "Rich?" 32

x

    Lifestyle Owners 33
    Legacy Builders 36
    Family Lifestyle/Family Legacy 38
    Family Legacies 39
    Coaching Lifestyle vs. Legacy 40
The Coaching Discovery Process 44

PART TWO: COACHING DISCOVERY
The Approach 47

7\. Setting the Ground Rules 49
    The Up Front Contract...49
    Conducting the Orchestra 50

8\. Speaking the Truth..53
    Digging Out the "Little Lie" 53
    Challenging Beliefs 55
    The Most Sensitive Subject..56
    Distinguishing Knowing and Not Knowing................59

9\. Asking Questions 61
    Start With an Observation..61
    Open Ended Questions..62
    Using Forms..63

10\. Listening...67
    One Mouth, Two Ears...67
    Sounds of Silence 69

11\. Coaching about Value..71
    The Valuation Obstacle 71
    Sellers "Lie" 72
    Valuations are Confusing..74
    What is a "Certified" Valuation?...................................75
    What is the "Right" Price? 77
    A Coaching Approach to Value Discussions..............79

12. Behavioral Profiling 81
    Communicating Effectively 81
    Recognizing Communications Style... 83
    Closing an Engagement 85
13. Nobody Likes a Showoff 87
    The Expertise Trap 87
    Coaching with Stories 89
The Coaching Discovery Approach 90

PART THREE: COACHING DISCOVERY
The Deliverables 93
14. The Owner's Initial Objective 95
    "I'll Just Sell It" 95
    The Path of Least Resistance 96
    Explaining the Odds 98
    Setting Client Expectations 100
15. The Personal Vision 103
    Visioning the Future 103
    Filling in Their Week 104
    Components of the Vision 106
    Practice, Practice, Practice 107
    Two "Good" Obstacles to Exit Planning Implementation 108
    "Death by Inattention" 108
    "Death by Over-Attention" 109
    Preventing the Two Obstacles 110
16. Delegation and Depth 111
    Owner Centricity 111
    The Small Business Start-Up 111
    It's the Management, Stupid! 113
    Reverse Depression 115
    Owner Centricity and Decision Addiction 115
17. Beyond Coaching 119

  The Next Phase 119
  Possible Financial Recommendations 119
  Possible Planning Recommendations 120
  Possible Revenue and Profit Recommendations 120
  Possible Operations Recommendations 121
  Closing the Implementation Engagement 122
18. It Takes a Team 123
  Coaching is One-on-one 123
  Building the Team 124
  Qualifying your Teammates 125
  The Impact of Bad Advice 127
  The Starters 129
  The Special Teams 130
  On the Sidelines 131
19. Leading the Team 133
  The Quarterback 133
  The Coach 133
  Acknowledging Your Position 134
  Working with Incumbents 136
  Referral Sources and Reciprocation 136
  Referral Fees 137
20. Stakeholders 139
  Other Stakeholders 139
  Ownership 139
  Other Internal Stakeholders 141
  External Stakeholders 142
  Don't Tell Anyone! 143
21. Internal Buyers 145
  Absentee Owners 146
  Selling to Employees 147
  Company Cash Flow 148

Time vs. Risk 149
22. You Can't Aways Get What You Want 151
Expectations 151
Who is Responsible? 152
Reality Bites 152
23. The Dismal Ds: Contingency and Continuity Planning 155
Planning - The Cure for the Dismal Ds 156
Business Continuity Instructions 158
Contingency vs. Continuity Planning 159
Continuity Planning 159
Buy/Sell or Shareholder Agreements 160
Trusted Advisors 162
Employee Compensation and Stay Bonuses 163
Working Capital and Credit Guarantees 164
Licenses 165
24. Life After the Business 167
Entrepreneurs Don't Have Rearview Mirrors 167
Visioning the Future 168
Leaping into the Void 169
Purpose 169
Identity 170
Activity 171
Thank You 172
The Coaching Discovery Deliverable 173

AFTERWARD:
Main Street or Middle-Market? 175
Main Street Businesses 175
Mom and Pop Businesses 176
Middle-Market Businesses 177

SOURCES: 179

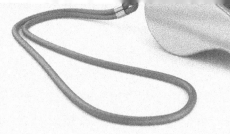

FORWARD:
We are on a Mission

> *"People don't care what you know, until they know that you care."*
> ~ Theodore Roosevelt

Our company, ExitMap®, has a mission. We are focused on going beyond helping business owners transition from their companies. We need them to be happy with the results. It isn't as easy as it may sound, if it was, this book wouldn't be necessary.

Two widely cited surveys of business owners found that one year following their exit from the business, over 75% of them were unhappy with or "regretted" the results.[1] Exit planners as a profession should be mortified by that statistic.

How would we judge a teacher whose students failed 75% of their subjects? Or a surgeon who had "only" 75% of his patients die on the operating table? Being less dramatic, what if 75% of the airline industry's flights arrived safely, but landed somewhere other than their advertised destination?

The last analogy is the most apt. When you look for the exit sign in a building, it's because you want to be somewhere else. (If the building is on fire, you probably just want to be anywhere else!) No one leaves a building without an idea of where they are going, even if it's just to get to the car. Where you are at the moment isn't fulfilling your purpose any longer. You want to go somewhere else for a reason.

Business owners who plan their exits should start with the end in mind. They need to have somewhere else that they want to go when they walk away. Unfortunately, too many are experiencing a milder version of the "building on fire" motivation. They are pretty sure that they don't want to run the company any longer, but they aren't sure what they want to do instead.

A substantial number of exit planning advisors cite the 75% statistic on their websites and a quick Google search will turn up over a dozen publications and advisor websites that quote it. When asked why the 75% are unhappy, most advisors will say, "That's because the owners didn't get enough money." (Note: The surveys did not ask for the reason why the owners were unhappy.)

That isn't true. The owners we work with generally have a pretty good idea of how much they need to retire. The only reason for an owner to be unhappy is if their planning didn't encompass a vision for their life after the exit. That is what every advisor should work hard to avoid.

Imagine you decide to exit a building. You ask a consultant for directions. He leads you to a door with a large red exit sign above. He opens the door for you. You step through, and it latches behind you.

You find yourself on a strange street in an unfamiliar city. You don't know anyone, and no one knows you. You don't know where to go next, or how to resolve your situation. It feels like a nightmare.

The consultant did what you asked. He showed you how to get out of the building, but did he help you accomplish your objective? That's what happens to too many business owners.

Our mission is to help their advisors coach them to a more fulfilling solution, one where the result is something they expect and gladly anticipate. It's a lot more than just showing them the door. It needs to start with Coaching Discovery.

Coaching Discovery is a phrase meant to have multiple applications.

Coaching Discovery as a <u>process</u> is a specific way of generating deeper conversations to gather the information needed to create a solid and comprehensive plan. It recognizes the difference in counseling business owners, and what it takes to build a stronger relationship with this specific type of client.

Coaching Discovery as an <u>approach</u> is the technique of coaching as a methodology. Think of figuratively moving from across the table to sitting side by side with the client. Instead of delivering answers, you set out on the journey of learning what the client wants together. He or she comes to the conclusions "on their own" with the coach testing and qualifying their conclusions.

Coaching Discovery as a <u>deliverable</u> is the concrete outcome of the process and the approach. It is a plan that will meet with little or no resistance from clients since it is clearly theirs from beginning to end.

This book focuses on how advisors, any advisors, can better serve their business owner clients by providing a little more coaching before they start giving advice. It is divided into three parts: the Process, the Approach and the Deliverable. The Process discusses the special considerations of dealing with business owners. The Approach focuses on your working relationship. The Deliverable concentrates on the nuts and bolts of developing a plan.

INTRODUCTION:
One professional to another

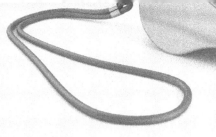

*"To be as good as they can be,
...they have to feel that you are part of them and they are part of you."*

~ Bobby Knight

As an author, I write my books as if I am speaking to the reader. I have a clear picture in my mind of who I think that is, but it differs from book to book.

In *11 Things You Absolutely Need to Know about Selling Your Business*, I was simply writing a pretty straightforward list of things small business owners needed to know before attempting the sale of a company. It's a short book (30,000 words) and the chapters are in the order of tasks the reader is likely to face.

For *Hunting in a Farmer's World: Celebrating the Life of an Entrepreneur*, I deliberately wanted to use a storytelling format. It is intended to read like a novel, with the readers/entrepreneurs able to see themselves as the protagonists. Like a novel, each chapter starts with a scenario, then elaborates on its details or impact. Each chapter ends with a lead in to the next chapter. I'm proud of all the awards the book received, but even more pleased by all the comments from folks who read the entire book in one sitting. I made the format and font smaller so it would look like a "little" book, but it's 55,000 words, or about the same length as the average novel.

Your Exit Map: Navigating the Boomer Bust is my attempt to bring new life to a topic that is well covered in other books, but (in my humble opinion) too densely informative for the typically ADD entrepreneur I profiled in *"Hunting."* We spent a lot of time selecting and creating the more than 300 pictures and illustrations that are on every page. It's not exactly a comic book, but it is closer to entertainment than to the detailed descriptions of legal and organizational requirements that fill the more common "how to" books. Again, my favorite comments are those that say reading it is like talking to me.

"You write just like you talk," has always been a compliment that puzzles me. How else should I write? I've always felt that my books should be a conversation between the reader and me. That's what made this book so difficult on the front end. Before I could start writing, I needed to find the appropriate "voice."

This book targets advisors to business owners. It's written as a conversation between professionals. I wanted to make it a "handbook." To that end, I chose a smaller format and larger type. My hope is that advisors will keep it around as a quick reference.

I tried several formats, including chapters for owners, and splitting it into discussions of soft skills and technical skills. I finally realized that none of those would be appropriate in a discussion between peers.

I finally scrapped the first 15 chapters and chose this "handbook" approach instead. I draw heavily on my own experience in over 25,000 hours of face-to-face coaching with about 500 business owners. This book is about coaching. Other authors do a better job of detailing value creation, operational improvement, tax planning, estate coordination and legal issues. While my exit planning practice deals with all of those things, my expertise lies in coaching business owners.

That's also a bit of a disclaimer. This book doesn't cover every nuance about exit planning. One of the reasons I love exit planning is because every solution is different. No two owners are the same. Their goals and objectives, the importance of lifestyle or legacy, and frequently both, are uniquely theirs.

You also might recognize one or two stories from my previous books. (If of course, you read them.) They are from my own experience or that of others, but they are real. Stories are the oldest and best way of conveying information. They are passed from person to person as the original newspaper or television.

If I have a story that helps to illustrate a specific point, I'm not ashamed to use it. I think it's a lot better than those "theoretical allegories" that start with, "Martin sat in his corner office thinking about what had happened in the meeting."

Some people like allegories. I like real life. It's where I work, and what I talk about.

The other major component in planning is the client's company. Its history, size, industry, markets, margins and management team aren't of themselves unique, but the combination of those factors is. We started the ExitMap® because most planning rightfully revolves around the owner, however, the company is the financial driver for the owner's objectives. Without considering it, most planning risks become irrelevant.

Put the two together and the possibilities are literally endless. Every exit plan has components that could apply to many owners and companies, but the final solution is always singular.

Coaching is different in every engagement, but the principles are the same. The more you know about the client, and the more your client trusts you, the better the results will be.

PART ONE: COACHING DISCOVERY
THE PROCESS

This book is dedicated to the concept of Coaching Discovery. The term is used throughout, but like many such combinations of words in the English language, it can have several meanings.

I recently saw a special about George Carlin. It called him the first semantic comedian. He loved examining the meaning of words, and so do I.

In one segment he compared *alter* and *change*. "You can alter your plans or change your plans," he said. "Both mean the same thing." "But if you alter your pants or change your pants, you are talking about two entirely different activities."

I think that coaching discovery is similar in its varied uses.

The **process** of coaching discovery, when "coaching" is a participle, focuses on the action of coaching to obtain the result of discovery. The process of discovery is where an advisor creates trust and builds the foundation for a long-term relationship. It is the most critical part of any engagement and the subject of Part One of the book.

The **approach** of coaching discovery uses the words more as a compound noun. Coaching as a noun is defined by the Cambridge Dictionary as "The act of giving special classes in…a work-related activity, especially to one person." This is the focus of Part Two - the actual delivery of coaching to a business owner.

The **deliverable** of coaching discovery is where coaching is used as an adjective to describe the type of discovery you are providing. The output of your work together is unique, since its creation is shared at every stage by the client, and the result is as much theirs as it is yours. The discovery process is experienced by the advisor side by side with the client. This is the topic of Part Three.

> All advisors engage in some form of coaching.

All advisors engage in some form of coaching, and although most don't consider that a separate skill set from their normal services, they should.

Many advisors approach business owners with the same processes and tools as they use with other clients. That's a mistake. Business owners are different. On average, they only represent about 3% of the working population.[2] They have typically committed decades to growing their businesses, and have a disproportionate percentage of their personal net worth invested in a company that is partially or wholly dependent on their presence.

Understanding why they think the way they do (see my book *Hunting in a Farmer's World; Celebrating the mind of an Entrepreneur,*) and tailoring your process to their needs, is key to your success as an advisor to them. Let's talk about the process of coaching discovery for business owners.

1. Coaching Before Advising

"You can lead a horse to water, but you can't make him drink."
A Dialogue Conteinyng The Nomber in effect of all the
Prouerbes in the English Tongue
~ John Heywood (1546)

Feeling the Rush

The typical business owner lives on dopamine. According to WebMD:
> Dopamine is a type of neurotransmitter. Your body makes it, and your nervous system uses it to send messages between nerve cells. That's why it's sometimes called a chemical messenger. Dopamine plays a role in how we feel pleasure. It's a big part of our unique human ability to think and plan.

That's what business owners do; they think and plan. Their lives are a chain of thought processes that go like this, "What if I do this? How will it affect the business? Then what would I do next? What would be the effect of that?"

An owner's brain is trained to generate dopamine. That, "What if? What if? What if?" chain is actually pleasurable. It uses the same neurotransmitter that is triggered by nicotine or alcohol, and the craving for that dopamine rush is the driving force of addiction.

Many owners complain that their employees can't make decisions and can't think critically. The problem is, they understand consciously that their businesses would run better if they groomed decision-makers, but unconsciously they are *addicted* to making decisions.

Every time an employee asks, "What should I do about this, boss?" there is a little rush. It's like an old cartoon. The good angel is sitting on one shoulder saying, "Make them go through the thought process themselves." The little horned devil is on the other shoulder saying, "Go ahead. Tell him just this once. It's faster, and it feels *good*."

Replacing this rush is also a major issue in adjusting to life after the business, but that will be addressed later, for now let's focus on the relationship between the client and the coach.

Advisors are frequently frustrated by a client's reluctance to implement their recommendations. They spend a lot of time and effort developing a course of action, and more time and effort explaining it to the client. The business owner client listens, agrees, and then does...nothing.

"I'm too busy running the business," is a frequent excuse. What is really happening is that the owner is too busy feeding their dopamine rush. Implementing someone else's decision is antithetical to what made them successful entrepreneurs in the first place.

> Owners are more likely to take action on their own decisions.

Owners are more likely to take action on their own decisions. That's why a coaching approach (where you ask more questions and the client supplies the answers,) is usually more effective than an advisory approach where you provide the client with all the answers.

The Advisory Rush

Most advisory professionals who work with business owners are business owners themselves. Some 80% of exit planners practice in firms of ten people or less, and over 75% are principals or partners in those firms.[3] They too are decision makers and, not surprisingly, get the same dopamine reaction as their clients when they give advice.

That's why coaching is a challenge for many advisors. They make the same excuses as the owner. Instead of complaining about employees who can't make their own decisions, they complain about clients who fail to implement their advice. They have the little cartoon angel saying, "Let the client decide." Their cartoon devil is saying, "Just give them the answer. That's what they hired you for. Besides, it feels *good*."

Some consultants take what I call the "Pro from Dover" approach. They charge hefty fees to tell the owner what he or she needs to do to be more successful. Those fees are justified by their briefcase or laptop full of answers.

I'm not saying that they aren't successful. Their client companies make more money and can sell for a lot higher value. The problem is that *75% say they are unhappy with the results a year later*. The client stated a goal, the consultants hit the target, and the client was temporarily happy. I can only presume that the 25% who are happy are very likely the ones that had "increasing the money in my pocket" as their prime directive.

I've worked with over 500 owners in my career. Some were clients for a few months and others for a few decades. I'm willing to concede that one in five might have been principally motivated by money. The large majority, however, were not.

They almost always list security for their families as the prime reason for growing a successful business. I acknowledge that money in the bank is a terrific security blanket, but many owners who are seeking an exit strategy already have enough to take care of most potential security threats.

Generational wealth is sometimes an objective, but not very often. Entrepreneurs are typically hard working. They want their children to have the advantages of a good education and a choice of careers, but few want to underwrite a life of idle amusement.

After family, employees and community are usually high on the owner's priority list. Money as merely a way of keeping score is fine, and most wouldn't mind a bit of luxury in their lives, but it isn't their main objective.

So why do so many advisors focus on the money as the primary factor in their planning?

To a Hammer...
Everything is a nail. I often use the analogy of a medical practice. A patient goes to a doctor and says, "Doctor, my shoulder hurts terribly. I can't stand it anymore. Can you help me?"

Of course, that's why the doctor studied medicine in the first place. A few do it just for the money, but most want to help people. The doctor will assure the patient that help is available, but what kind of help depends a lot on what kind of doctor the patient chose to see.

If the patient is visiting an Internist, a course of anti-inflammatories might be the next step. If it's an Orthopedic surgeon, surgery is much more likely to be in the treatment plan. A Chiropractor is certain to try manipulation, and an Acupuncturist will get out the needles.

Each will treat the shoulder pain. All will likely deliver results. The patient will probably never realize that the treatment was determined by the type of practitioner he selected, not by any canon of best practices for shoulder pain.

A similar thing often happens when a business owner selects someone to help with their exit planning. An accountant is likely to build the plan around preferential tax treatment. An attorney might focus on asset protection or contracts with key employees. In the National Exit Planners Survey™, attorneys and accountants cited, "Client had already received an offer for the business," as the most frequent reason their advice is sought.

Business consultants specialize in improving operations and profitability. Increasing the value of the business helps in a lot of areas, but we've already established that it doesn't necessarily meet the client's life objectives.

A few years ago, I ran into a business broker that I've known for a long time. His approach was simple. If an owner would agree to offer 100% seller financing of the sale, he would list the business and facilitate the transaction. (Need I mention that he never financed his commission?)

He proudly showed me his new business cards. He had added "Exit Planner" next to "Business Broker" under his name. I asked him how he handled exit planning. "Easy," he said, "If they will accept 100% seller financing, I'll help them exit their business."

To a hammer, everything is a nail.

That's why the main challenge in coaching isn't the client. *It's the advisor*. And it is why this book isn't aimed at getting business owners to hire a coach. It's directed to advisors who can and want to serve their clients better by delivering a little more coaching before they offer their advice.

> That's why the main challenge in coaching isn't the client.

What is Coaching Skill?

Let's make it simple. Coaching is asking questions. An experienced football coach will ask the questions that no one else does, preferably in a way that doesn't offend the quarterback or his teammates.

Do you want to win the game? Do you think everyone on the team wants to win the game? Do you think anyone would prefer to *lose* the game?

The exit planning coach should utilize a similar approach.

Do you want to save money on taxes? Do you want to maintain control until you are paid what the company is worth? Do you want to ensure that your family is taken care of?

These aren't the questions that derail a transition plan. Here are a few that, left unasked, will.

- Is there something more important to you than the proceeds from selling?
- Is there a part of your legacy that must be preserved if at all possible?
- Are there non-financial or non-equity stakeholders whose welfare must figure into the plan?
- Is your family on board with this?
- Are there key employees whose participation is critical to success?

These are the questions that an advisor who is only focused on the technical complexities of exiting or the amount of the proceeds will often omit.

The Most Important Question
What will you do when you no longer own this business?

For many entrepreneurs, that's the stumper. Unless your client can answer it clearly and comfortably, your plan is very likely to fail. Failure is when an owner regrets their exit after the transfer. The owner should be excited, and happy to leave the business ownership phase of life in the rearview mirror.

> The owner should be excited, and happy to leave the business.

Many advisors will ask it in a casual way, "So what will you do next?" *They* may react little or not at all if the response *is* "I don't know." Or, if an owner laughingly says, "I'm going to play a lot of golf." The advisor writes down "play a lot of golf," in the space reserved for life planning after the business and moves on.

When I was active as a business broker, I would decline a listing if an owner couldn't enunciate a plan for life after the business. In my first book, *11 Things You Absolutely Need to Know about Selling Your Business*, I describe a case where an owner declined two offers, each for twice his company's estimated value. He simply didn't know what he would do next, and chose to keep on working rather than have to face that decision.

"I don't know" is a signal that the owner can't envision life without the activity of the business. Another common answer is, "I'll figure it out after I get out of here." Which is almost always too late.

I've had many a retired owner tell me, "I never thought I could play too much golf."

According to the surveys by the Exit Planning Institute and PwC cited in the forward to this book, over 75% of former business owners are unhappy with their exits one year after selling.

I don't know of any of our clients who are in the "75% unhappy with the results" group. Some get less than they expected, and for others it takes longer than they hoped, but when they have exited, they understand the how, why and what of the process. The outcome is what they expected, although it may not always be what they hoped for.

Perhaps that's just luck, but I like to think it's at least partially due to coaching. The technical and financial complexities of a successful transition are nothing to sneeze at, but helping an owner be prepared is so much more than that.

The coach of any team knows more plays than the players. He or she allocates the resources, and recommends what play to run next. Once the players take the field, however, the coach can only watch. How the coach prepares them before the game is 90% of the job.

It sounds simple, but the need for coaching skill evades many advisors, only to their client's detriment.

> Once the players take the field, the coach can only watch.

2. Why Coaching Owners is Different

"Don't ever ask a player to do something he doesn't have the ability to do. He'll just question your ability as a coach, not his as an athlete."

~ Lou Holtz

There are a number of reasons why coaching business owners differs from coaching other executives. "Coaching" for our purposes is defined by any advisory activity intended to help a client make better decisions. It consists more of asking questions than rendering actual professional opinions and can be practiced by any professional advisor.

Accountants, attorneys, and consultants all coach, even when they aren't consciously doing so. If you understand why the advice given to an owner is different, you'll have more success in getting their cooperation.

The Buck Stops Here

All executives are decision-makers. Owners are bound to live by the outcomes of their decisions, regardless of whether they are good or bad. Most are painfully aware of the "what if" scenarios that stemmed from their last wrong decision. As a client once told me, "I've learned so *little* from my successes."

> *"I've learned so little from my successes."*

Hopefully, this creates some balance between a tendency to move forward throwing caution to the wind and the self-restraint that comes from having your own livelihood on the line.

My friend Larry Linne, the author of *Make the Noise Go Away*, tells a great (if apocryphal) story. In a company that sells large, expensive manufacturing equipment, the Vice President of Sales is responsible for checking all the outgoing quotes. One day he walks into the owner's office and asks for a meeting. The owner agrees, and the executive closes the door. As we all know, that's never a good sign.

The executive is clearly miserable. "Boss," he begins, "You know that big order we just got from Amalgamated International?" Of course the owner knows. It's the biggest sale they've had this year. "Well, I was just going over the contract for installation, and realized I missed the fact that the sales rep didn't include our labor costs on the job."

"How bad is it?" the owner asked. "We are going to have to eat a half-million dollars," was the response. "I know that it's my job to review this, and I don't know how I could have missed something that big. I understand if you want my resignation."

The owner thinks about it. Then he explains that the vice president gained his position because of his talent. It's a tremendous error, and the company will have a pretty bad year because of it. Of course there will be no bonus, but otherwise they will have to chalk it up to a learning experience. It makes no sense to fire his most talented salesperson over a single mistake.

The employee thanks the owner for his understanding, and promises that he will never, ever fail to carefully review an order again. He slinks out of the office, but as he walks down the hall, he regains the spring in his step and his shoulders straighten. A huge weight has just been taken off of them.

After he leaves, the owner puts his elbows on the desk and sinks his head into his hands. He will have to tap into the credit line to make payroll for the next quarter, and the loss will put a dead stop to his expansion plans. The company will survive, but it isn't going to be much fun for a while.

It's My Money
Executives have budgets. They can exceed their budgets, but are seldom capable of bringing down the whole company. Achieving their goals may bring a bonus, but only in proportion to their impact on the entire organization.

Owners have profit. It's not just a target, but actual personal income. Every expenditure, every hire, represents a reduction in the profit. For founder-owners, I've never seen that linkage go away, even if the company may have grown to hundreds of employees. It often makes them very cautious of committing to new ideas, even when they are promising. A coach should be prepared to defend new ideas against the innate caution of standing pat.

A banker friend who has worked with small business owners throughout his career once told me, "I can understand everything about their businesses. I comprehend how they create income, and what their critical performance factors are. I have a great feeling for what worries them. However, I will never, ever, have the terror that comes with making a mistake or the sick feeling in the pit of my stomach that comes with a problem that threatens their whole existence."

Ironically, owners can't communicate that to employees. Even if their workers are empathetic, the personal nature of the terror is theirs alone. If they said things like "Your mistakes are taking money out of my pocket," or "If I give you a raise my family won't be able to go on vacation," they would be considered crass and venal.

It's My Baby
There are few bonds as deep as that of an owner towards his or her company. Everything has the owner's imprint on it. The building that the business is in, the furniture the employees use, the methods, products, systems, slogans, logo, procedures, marketing, branding, web presence, and target customers were frequently all created or chosen by the owner.

Before suggesting any change, the coach must remember something. *The owner made what he or she thought was the best decision depending on the resources and conditions at the time.* Perhaps the finances or personnel were unavailable then. There could be new

> There are few bonds as deep as that of an owner towards his or her company.

competition. Maybe the market has changed. None of these things mean that the owner made a bad decision previously.

Before recommending change, a coach should always ask about what came before. Have conditions changed? Have the owner's objectives changed? Whatever the current situation, it isn't the same as it was previously.

When you are coaching a business owner, you are not just advising an executive businessperson. You are dealing with the executive. Keep in mind the special connection between a business and its owner in order to deliver the most effective coaching advice.

Coaches speak the truth, but you have to use some common sense. Telling a mother that her baby is ugly will not only win you no friends, but it isn't going to change anything. You won't have a client, and the baby will still be ugly.

It's My Decision

I'm not going to belabor the point. We've discussed the dopamine of decision making and the possessive attitude toward "my" business. The decisions made for the business, if they are to have the slightest chance of implementation, must be made by the owner, not you.

That is why the analysis tools in ExitMap® are all designed to be completed together with the owner. If you are the type of advisor that prefers to go into a room, work alone, and return to the client with a completed plan, they aren't for you.

I would also be curious about the long-term satisfaction of your clients.

When I was working on my MBA at Pepperdine, we had a lecture from a Japanese CEO. He discussed Ringi, the bottom-up process of decision making in Japanese organizations. He showed us how many iterations of a strategy were run through the management team before committing to a plan.

One of my classmates (all were executives, mostly in large corporations) asked about the commitment of time. In the current environment, he argued, speed of decision making was critical. (It doesn't matter how long ago this was, the same argument is used today.) The CEO laughed.

"It isn't the speed of decision making that is important," he said, "It's the speed of implementation."

> *"It isn't the speed of decision making that is important. It's the speed of implementation."*

"We laugh at American CEOs who are so proud of pointing to their decision making as a sign of leadership. We watch them hand down edicts, and then spend months or years trying to get their organizations to make them happen."

"Yes, we spend a comparatively long time reaching a decision. When we do, however, everyone understands the reasons for it, the logic behind it, and their role in making it happen. Implementation isn't another phase; it is the immediate and direct result of announcing the decision."

I think Ringi is very applicable to exit planning. Unless an owner has bought into every step of the decision making process, they are unlikely to implement your recommendations without another whole phase of selling your ideas.

3 "I am Not a Coach!"

> *"A common mistake ... is spending a disproportionate amount of time on "x's and o's" as compared to time learning about people."*
> ~ Mike Krzyzewski

Of course you are a coach. We've become far too enamored with "credentials." Everyone is a certified this or a certified that. We depend on other people to say whether we are qualified to do something. We depend on regulatory bureaucrats to put their seal of approval on everything. According to the Brookings Institution, occupational licensing is now required for almost 30% of all American jobs.[4]

Doctors, attorneys, accountants and teachers can create considerable harm if they are incompetent. And although licensing by itself doesn't guarantee competence, it makes sense for some professions.

How much regulatory oversight is needed for ballroom dance instructors, hair braiders, interior designers and upholsterers? Why does the state of Michigan require 1,460 *days* of training to become certified as an Athletic Trainer, but only 26 *hours* to be an Emergency Medical Technician?

I am not opposed to regulatory oversight. In the interest of full disclosure, I hold two degrees and seven business certifications, but none of them is in coaching. Yet I have over 25,000 hours of coaching business owners, some of whom have companies with 9-figure revenues and have been clients for over two decades. If I am unqualified, they would be very disappointed by the discovery.

A certification is a valuable indicator that shows if someone is committed to being a professional in a given area. It often serves as a "badge" of a specific qualification, but the simple fact of obtaining a certificate is not a guaranty of experience. For our purposes, coaching is a component of advisory competence, not a discreet discipline of its own.

Everyone in an advisory discipline is a coach. You are a coach when you are asking the client questions. You are a consultant when you are providing the client with answers.

> **You are a coach when you are asking the client questions. You are a consultant when providing the client answers.**

You are a consultant when you are working on things. You are a coach when you are working with people. You are a consultant when you are doing the work. You are a coach when you are helping someone else do the work.

Preparing tax returns is consulting. Asking the questions that involve proactive tax planning, business structures and asset protection is coaching.

Drafting legal documents is consulting. Asking why they are needed, and how they will be used, is coaching.

Allocating a client's liquid assets to different securities or investment vehicles is consulting. Asking about the client's life goals and concerns is coaching.

Showing a client the differing avenues to transition, whether selling to a third party, to employees or to family, is consulting. Asking why they want to leave the business, and what they want to happen with their lives afterwards, is coaching.

I often refer to "technical" advisors. Those are the skilled professionals who choose to focus on their consulting skills when dealing with a client. It's understandable. The client retained them for their advice. Many feel that they best serve the client by giving advice.

Hopefully, the remainder of this book will explain why your advice will be more impactful, more accurate, and more fulfilling if you ask some coaching questions first.

Here are the basic tenets of exit plan coaching:

1. Exit planning requires a team.
2. Every team needs a coach.
3. Every player can't be the coach.
4. The team needs to accept the coach.
5. The coach needs to accept the responsibility for coaching.

The coach position is one of responsibility. You are accepting the overarching responsibility for the performance of the team.

> The coach position is one of responsibility.

That requires you to ask questions, not only pertaining to your own specialty or expertise, but also the questions that others on the team may not be asking.

4. My Clients Hate the Word Exit."

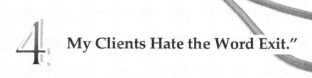

"It is easier to move from failure to success than from excuses to success."
~ John C. Maxwell

Let's begin by addressing the elephant in the room. I am an Exit Planner. My company sells exit planning tools to advisors. We conduct the annual National Exit Planners Survey™. The ExitMap® suite of coaching tools uses the word "exit" on virtually every page.

Advisors tell us regularly, "I like your materials, but can you remove the term 'exit?' It frightens my clients. They don't like to think of it that way."

Believe me, I understand. Anyone selling life insurance or funeral pre-planning knows that you don't start with, "So, let's discuss what happens when you DIE." For business owners, leaving the business is a little bit like death. That's why black humor in the exit planning world goes like this, "There are seven ways to exit your business. Six of those are head first."

Your client's company has been the central focus of his or her life for twenty or thirty years, and perhaps more. It is so ingrained in their persona and self-identification, that it's frightening for them to think of that part of their identity disappearing.

When Bob leaves home each day to run Bob's Widgets, he puts on the cloak of owner. He walks in the door of the business as the head honcho, *el jefe*, the final word, the boss. He never takes that cloak off. He might go out for a beer with employees after work, but he never

> *"There are seven ways to exit your business.*
> *Six of those are head first."*

becomes just one of the guys (especially when the table check comes). They are careful about what they say around him, and he self-censures his conversations with them.

Just as importantly, that cloak doesn't come off in his personal life either. He is Bob, the owner of Bob's Widgets, everywhere he goes. At the kids' sporting activities he is asked to sponsor ("It would be good for your business!") In his church, at the Chamber of Commerce, and at parties he is introduced as "Bob, the owner of Bob's Widgets."

He overhears the identification at family gatherings. "Oh, that's Sally's cousin Bob. He owns his own business." When his friends discuss their jobs, a bad boss, pending layoffs, or a reorganization they say, "Of course you don't have to worry about these things, Bob. You own the company." (Ah, if they only knew…)

> So the word "exit" has a finality that jars a lot of clients.

So the word "exit" has a finality that jars a lot of clients. Advisors use lots of alternatives, like transition, succession or continuation - all of which imply an ongoing process, albeit one that doesn't include the owner. Why would an advisor use the term "Exit" at all if it could be avoided?

We use it because a coach is a trusted advisor, and a trusted advisor always speaks the truth. Not some of the time. Not just when it is agreeable. Not when it can't be avoided. *All of the time.* The coaching relationship should be comfortable, but not too comfortable.

I use exit to describe the final outcome of an implemented business plan. It usually involves a transaction, with legal documentation of a sale or other transfer mechanism. It can include detailed succession planning for family members or a management team. We often discuss continuation – what happens if the plan is accelerated by unfortunate circumstances. Retirement might have a place in the conversation, or it might be leading to a "second act" or pursuing your life's passion.

But all those terms, whether synonyms or euphemisms, are encompassed in the word "exit." We might as well get that on the table from the outset. If you start the advisory process by ducking anything that a client finds uncomfortable, you aren't serving your purpose as a coach.

Let's agree to call a business transition what it is. Whether an owner wants to sell the business to a third party, create a family legacy through his or her children, finance a leveraged buy out to employees, or just close down in an orderly manner, the ultimate objective is to exit.

> If you start the advisory process by ducking things that a client finds uncomfortable, you aren't serving your purpose as a coach.

Business owners are tough. They may not love the term, but they'll get over it.

5. "I Don't need a Coach"

> *"A coach is someone who tells you what you don't want to hear, who has you see what you don't want to see, so you can be who you have always known you could be."*
>
> ~ Tom Landry

Every owner needs a coach. In fact, anyone who wants to really excel at anything has a coach.

Professional athletes earn millions of dollars for playing games. They clearly know how to throw, catch, hit, run, or perform the other functions of their profession. In fact, they can do it better than 99.99% of the entire population of the rest of world.

> Anyone who wants to really excel at anything has a coach.

So why do they have coaches? Not just a single coach, but specialists in every area of performance. They have people who observe their shot or their swing on a daily basis. The coaches warn them when they are drifting from their most effective form. They try new ideas, especially for better conditioning (even though most are physically conditioned at a level that is only fantasy for the rest of us).

During the off season, many seek out *more* coaching. You've heard it numerous times from broadcasters in every sport. "He spent the off season working with (famous coach or trainer's name) to improve his (pick a skill)."

Have you ever had a child who was good at a sport, or even just loved the sport, whether excellence was part of the equation or not? What did you do? If you are like most middle-class parents, you probably hired a coach. If your child was good enough to cause visions of a possible college scholarship, you definitely hired a coach.

There are a number of reasons business owners resist hiring a coach.

For one thing, the term "business coach" is ill-defined. What *should* a coach do?

Business coaching has become more widely accepted in the twenty-first century. It's no longer embarrassing for a corporate executive to mention that he or she has a coach. In many large organizations, it is expected and taken as a sign that the company thinks you are worth investing in. For entrepreneurs however, acceptance has been considerably slower and carries with it a negative connotation in many minds.

Let's go back to Bob at Bob's Widgets. He is accustomed to being the answer man. Every issue that can't be resolved by managers (no matter how large the company is) percolates up to him. Admitting to the employees that he doesn't know everything can be embarrassing. Because who could possibly know more about running the company than Bob?

Just because someone has a business card that says "coach" doesn't mean they are the one you need. Just as in sports, a good coach specializes in a service offering, and can clearly state what that offering is. What area of the business will their coaching improve?

To start, coaching is a two-way street. For every coach there must be a coachee. The title infers a one-to-one or one-to-many relationship between human beings. As the skill becomes more widely accepted, some advisors simply use the term to appear more current, not because they provide actual coaching services.

A professional who is going to review your business processes, marketing, branding, financial controls or logistics is a business consultant. Their interaction with people is secondary to the application of their expertise. As the quote from Tom Landry suggests, a coach is someone who helps the client be better. They don't take the field and throw the ball for them.

> A coach is someone who helps the client be better.

Some coaches are specialists and are clear about their expertise. Coaching salespeople and/or sales managers is an easily identifiable specialty. Leadership or management development coaching is another.

Some coaches are specialists in facilitation, which is essentially coaching for groups. They may lead team building, strategic planning sessions or annual retreats. Some coach management teams on accountability, goal setting or prioritization. Three systems in broad use, EOS, Scaling Up and Value Builder, are all versions of this team coaching approach.

I've coached business owners, and only business owners, for the last 30 years. Outside of my exit planning practice, I still do "general" business coaching for a few dozen CEOs. In these cases, the coaching can take many forms. They aren't looking for someone to "teach" them how to run an organization. They all do that quite well already. Their coaching sessions usually fall into a few categories.

- Reviewing their stated goals for themselves and/or the company
- Following up on priorities
- Updating an (often lengthy) "to-do" list of issues they need to check on regularly
- Discussing alternative approaches to personnel or customer issues
- Lending my experience (and by osmosis, that of hundreds of previous clients) to their analysis of operational challenges
- Helping them envision the future of the business, and what resources it will take to get there
- Acting as "devil's advocate" to poke holes in a new idea or plan
- Support - reminding them that they do most things pretty well most of the time

Note that none of these categories include, "Telling them how to run their company." As Landry says, my job is to tell them what they don't want to hear and see what they don't want to see. I don't personally implement or solve any of the issues enumerated above. Actual results are only realized if they come from the quarterback. That's the business owner.

A coach is a truth-sayer. The client's employees may be both bright and experienced, but at the end of the day their paycheck depends on their continued employment. They may offer suggestions, but they seldom get in the boss's face. Family is there for support, but cannot provide candid criticism. Peers, other business owners, may be helpful (most of my coaching clients also participate in business owner peer groups), but few will share their very deepest fears or failures in front of a group.

> The coach fills the gaps between consultants, employees, family and peers.

The coach fills the gaps between consultants, employees, family and peers. They are the listening post, mirror, and confidant.

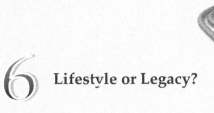
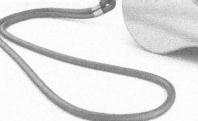

6. Lifestyle or Legacy?

"Winning is a habit. Unfortunately, so is losing."
~ Vince Lombardi

What Kind of Owner are You Coaching?

There are three types of business owners. The first kind, which encompasses the vast majority of small businesses, is the one who simply wants to make a living from running his or her business. They dream of the day that they can take vacations without worrying about the impact on their companies. Sometimes their biggest goal is to go home at five o'clock, or just to limit their work week to five days.

This type of owner has a job, not a business. Their best potential for exit is to convince an employee to take over their job.

But if they are tenacious, if they execute on their plans and are able to groom good employees, eventually they might join the owners who can take a good living for granted. Those are the other two types of owners, and as a coach, you have to determine whether their goals are focused on a lifestyle or a legacy.

Both lifestyle and legacy owners would be considered successful, in the sense that they are financially secure, expect to retire at a time of their choosing, and barring mishaps, should be able to enjoy that retirement doing what they wish. However, they run their businesses very differently.

Legacy builders and lifestyle owners both, exist in manufacturing, distribution, professional services and every other type of industry.

> Legacy builders see their companies and their lives as having an objective that is more than just financial success.

Figuring out which is which has a lot to do with personal vision, but legacy builders aren't typically driven by a bigger paycheck. They see their companies and their lives as having an objective that is more than just financial success.

What is "Rich?"
First, let's define wealth, since the perception of wealth is a substantial part (although not by any means all) of the difference. Some years ago my family was skiing at Deer Valley, Utah. For those of you who haven't been there, Deer Valley is a beautiful resort. It's one of those that was developed as a ski resort, not as a ski mountain that eventually generated other development nearby. That means, like a golf resort, prime home sites were incorporated near the ski runs for those who could pay a premium for the location.

As you go up the main lift, the homes along the lift line are lush. Some are breathtaking. Three, four and five stories tall, 20,000 square feet or more, with indoor pools on separate glassed-in floors that are integrated into the main structure. I can't even estimate the prices, but you can be sure that they are astronomical.

My younger son, who was 13 or so at the time, gaped at some of the houses as we went up. He turned to me in the chair and said, "Dad, what is rich? Friends come to our house and say, "Boy, you are rich!" but you say we aren't. The people who own these houses (he first thought they were small hotels) are clearly rich. What is rich?"

I took a few hours to formulate a response. That night over dinner I replied. "Son, in your public high school you have many classmates whose parents work hard at a job just to provide the necessities. When they come to our house (an older, rambling 5 bedroom on a suburban acre) it is much more than they have, so they think we are rich."

"There are three kinds of rich. The first is well-to-do. That's what we are. We go out to dinner in a restaurant not just for special occasions, but whenever we don't feel like cooking. On vacations we fly to visit other countries, or to do fun things like ski or swim. If we need a new car, or something big fixed around the house, we just do it and don't have to worry too much about being able to pay for it. But your mother and I both have to work very hard in our business to afford our lifestyle."

"The second kind of rich we will call "wealthy." That's when you can live like we do, but you don't have to go to work every day to make it possible."

"The third kind of rich we'll call "escape velocity." (I think that term was coined by Bill Gates.) That's when you can pretty much do anything you want every day, and when you go to sleep you still have more money than when you woke up."

It's important to understand the attitude of your client towards wealth. I've worked with owners of companies that had less than $1,000,000 in revenue. If their income hit six figures in any given year, they thought they were rich. Others I know made six figures every month, but felt that they fell well short of wealthy, because they still had to run a company to make it happen.

> It is important to understand the attitude of your client towards wealth.

Overshooting or underestimating a client's mental impression of income can shake their faith in your ability to help them. In the case of someone who feels a six figure income is rich, saying that you can help him make "real" money would insult them terribly. With the person who feels the need to work is a disqualifier for real success, any indication that they really didn't "need" more money may give them the impression that you couldn't grasp their objectives.

Lifestyle Owners
Lifestyle business owners have reached the first kind of rich or are approaching it. Legacy builders are seeking much more, and it isn't merely about money. (Escape velocity usually requires favorable outside factors that few business owners can completely control. We call that luck.)

A few years ago I was on a judging panel for a business award. One of the finalists told her story of how she struggled and labored to build her company. I was getting impressed, until she mentioned that she hadn't turned a profit until her 13th year in business. Fortunately, she said, her husband was a prominent surgeon, and they could afford to absorb her losses indefinitely.

That's not a business, it's a hobby. She had a lifestyle, but not a lifestyle business.

I'm also not talking about the fantasy businesses that regularly grace the pages of Inc. Magazine, Entrepreneur, and Fast Company. You know, those stories that read like a mash-up between People magazine and the Whole Earth Catalog. Where the business owners live in a mountain top retreat, go kayaking with their employees on Tuesdays and Fridays, and sell imported herbal teas on the Internet. I envy them, but the number of such businesses are limited. Most of us are in far more plebeian environments, where the business requires hard work and regular attention.

My definition of a lifestyle business is one that allows the owner to live the life he or she wants. The business isn't integral to their lifestyle, as with the mountain-top tea seller's. It is any business that generates the income they need to achieve their personal vision, and runs well enough to give them sufficient time to spend that income any way they choose. It can be any business, as long as it is one that can be separated from their personal life.

I've observed that most founders of small businesses are seeking a lifestyle business. Their dreams include some baseline achievements like financial security for their families, the ability to retire in comfort, and a few weeks of vacation without calling in every day to run the company remotely. I think those are the trip wires for defining the beginning of a lifestyle business.

Those basics are really just the criteria for any well-run business. It has to go a bit further than that for a business to truly achieve "lifestyle" status. It mostly revolves around coming and going as you please. Depending on your interests, it may be working a four day week, or leaving at 3:00, or taking the children to school each day before coming in. Of course, in order to qualify, the owner can't be overwhelmed when they return to the office as the price of their "free" time.

It also has to fund not only their immediate and future financial needs, but also generate sufficient excess to let them indulge in their chosen activities without sacrificing elsewhere. Private schools are a quality choice, not an economic decision. Recreation destinations are determined by the activity desired, without worrying about time, distance, equipment or cost. Physical fitness regimens are scheduled each day or week, and the business simply has to fit (pun intended) around them.

If you are not in the office, your phone doesn't ring with problems; they are handled in the normal course of operations. If you say that you are going out, no one is worried about when you'll be back. If the business has an off month, it doesn't affect your paycheck. When you want information on how the business is running, it is available instantly, preferably on your smart phone.

One owner I know worked hard in his business for years. He was both creative and fascinated with new technology. Eventually he began integrating his hobby into the business, using new tech to automate systems and management processes. It worked so well that he bought a mountain home in another state, in the town he grew up in.

He left a manager in charge of the business and spent most of his time hunting and fishing. The business no longer grew, and eventually began to shrink, but it still threw off a decent income. Eventually he had to fly back on a regular basis to clean up accumulated issues, but as soon as things were stabilized again, he was back on an airplane to his hunting and fishing retreat. He continues this back-and-forth scenario today.

He assumes that he will eventually be approached by an acquirer, or the business will decline to the point where it makes more sense to close. He is fine with either outcome. It won't affect his lifestyle.

For the vast majority of small business owners, this situation could be the description of perfection. I work with a number of entrepreneurs who have achieved this or are close to it. But I also work with many who are well past this point, yet continue pushing the envelope to make the business grow. These are the Legacy owners and coaching them through a transition is very different.

Legacy Builders

Legacy owners are those who have achieved Lifestyle status but continue to work hard to build their businesses. Their objective is a company that does far more than merely provide a comfortable lifestyle and assure retirement. They have a vision that encompasses a life for the business beyond their own, or a purpose outside the business that requires funding.

The typical Legacy Builder runs a business that is very capable of continuing its day-to-day activities independently and indefinitely. Operations, management and sales are handled by competent employees. In fact, each is probably better than the owner at his or her specific responsibility. These owners are in the top 1% of American incomes. That income varies widely, but the top 1% is a minimum of about $500,000 a year.[5] The Legacy owner nonetheless chooses to work a full (40 hour plus) week to continue developing and improving the business, and not incidentally adding to its profit.

The Legacy owner is clearly not obsessive-compulsive, a workaholic, or in any other way driven unwillingly to work beyond common sense. It's easy for observers (and sometimes family) to accuse the Legacy owner of being enslaved to the job and unable to tear away for a personal life. That isn't true at all. The Legacy owners I am describing spend time with family and other pursuits. They coach Little League, attend recitals, and are active in the community. They take nice vacations (usually with family), and live in nice homes (often several of them), but are seldom ostentatious.

They are Legacy owners because they have an eye for a target that is beyond merely running a successful business. They have a bigger picture; a larger objective in mind. Developing an organization that lives beyond their own careers is at the core of their strategy, but it isn't just monument-building that drives them. It is what that organization as an engine of change can accomplish.

Some are motivated by the benefit to the community that their talent can deliver. More jobs employing more people who can provide security for their families. For some their own family is the motivation. They seek to change the lifestyle of their children, and their children's children, permanently (or at least for the next few generations).

For others it is even a greater community responsibility, the money to form a foundation, or to fund worthwhile causes.

I worked with one owner who had been removed from his mother by the state as a young child and was raised in a foster home. He was fortunate, and at 18 (when foster aid is cut off) attended a public college on scholarship. He then landed a position in a corporate management training program.

> Legacy owners have an eye for a target beyond merely running a successful business.

Eventually he started his own company and grew it to over 500 employees. He was very conscious of his ability to impact lives, and his workers received unusually good pay and benefits for the industry. When a buyer came along, however, he had no problem selling the company.

He had already started a foundation providing bus passes and cell phones to help kids who aged out of the foster system. Eventually it grew to add housing and educational assistance. He was already building a legacy, and expanding that was his primary objective. The money he made from running a substantial business was just a vehicle, and he never hesitated when the opportunity to expand that legacy came along.

Most Lifestyle owners say that they want to reach Legacy levels, but few actually do.

Family Lifestyle/Family Legacy

There are certain family businesses that have components of both lifestyle and legacy.

I grew up in the New York City metropolitan area. Where I lived, "diversity" meant a mixed population of those from German, Italian, Irish or Polish ancestors. Most people there had a clear idea of how and when their family came to the United States. As a result, I gained a lifelong interest in how immigrants adjust to life in their new country.

In New York there were a lot of greengrocers, the small shops that sold fresh fruit and vegetables. Today there aren't as many, but a substantial number of them still exist. They usually have stands of produce on display on the sidewalk in front of the store and a limited selection of dry goods inside. They are typically open from early morning until late at night.

For immigrant families, it's a great business. The margins don't allow a lot of room for payroll, but family members can work cheaply. Dad is at the wholesale market in the wee hours of the morning buying the day's produce inventory. Mom runs the store during the day. The kids clean up and straighten the stock after school, and grandma is at the register late in the evening. It's hard work, but a family can make a living.

In the 1920s and 1930s, many if not most greengrocers were owned by Polish and Italian immigrants. By the 1940s ownership had passed to Jews from Eastern Europe who were facing increasing discrimination in their native countries.

In the 1970s the predominant ethnicity of ownership was Korean. By the 1990s they were transitioning to folks from the Middle East.

What caused these transfers? The incoming owners were clearly buying a lifestyle. There are few language or educational barriers to owning a greengrocer. But the hard-working immigrants weren't buying a *permanent* lifestyle. They were buying a legacy. They wanted a better life for their children, and the business could provide it.

So as each generation put kids through college, they exited the business. Doctors and lawyers aren't interested in running a fruit stand, but that was okay. The business had served its purpose, as it did for the generations that came before and those that followed.

This example is one where literally thousands of people knew why they were buying a business and what they expected from it. The family lifestyle supported the family legacy. Unfortunately, there are many other cases where the two objectives are in conflict.

Family Legacies
As a coach, one of the most sensitive issues to deal with is family succession. An owner has built a successful business. It provides a very comfortable lifestyle for his or her family. Often, the owner expects the child or children to continue the legacy and run the business for the next generation.

That is often such a bad idea that there are any number of cliches about it. "Shirtsleeves to shirtsleeves in three generations" is the most common. According to a study by Cornell University, 40% of family-owned businesses are passed to a second generation. Only 13% have a third generation of ownership, and the fourth generation is involved only 3% of the time.[6]

In addition, many first-generation owners believe that the company should continue to provide for *all* of the children, whether they are involved in its operation or not. They refuse to accept that the sons shouldn't share profits with the daughters, or the oldest shouldn't contribute to the support of younger siblings.

Coaching for family enterprises is far more complex than we can address in this book. There are plenty of practical questions. Do the children want to run the business, or has it just been assumed since they were young? Are they capable of running the business? Are there key employees who are vital to operations, and who are willing to work under the offspring? Is the credit (and the credibility) of the business dependent on the parent(s)?

I was once interviewed by a couple who wanted assistance transferring their business to a son. They were very candid about their situation.

They had little in the way of savings, partially because they had been paying the son an outsized salary for years. They needed him to take the reins of the company and continue to pay them an income for the rest of their lives. However, there were a few issues.

He seldom came to work. He was nominally in charge of a moribund division, where the employees had threatened to resign if they actually had to deal with him. He spent company money without permission, and for things that had little or nothing to do with the business. He had never had any responsibility for the main areas of the business and showed no interest in learning.

They said, they would be willing to pay me handsomely if I could "straighten him out" and thus secure their retirement. Sadly, I had to decline the engagement.

I told them the story of the greengrocers. Sometimes a business has a lifespan, and it is difficult for a founder to recognize. My advice to them was to sell the business and retire as well as they were able on the proceeds.

Unfortunately, that would mean no income for the son, and to the parents it inferred a future role of permanent support. Eventually, and to the benefit of the parents, a younger son became interested in the business. Today he employs his older brother as a salesman. I suspect that was part of his deal.

Coaching Lifestyle vs. Legacy
Recently a client told me "You are wrong. I have a lifestyle business that is ALSO a legacy business." Sorry, but that doesn't fly outside of the type of family enterprises I just described.

He has built a good company and continues to improve it, but he is not driving to make it into something that carries on beyond him. His objective is to (eventually) make it large enough to be acquired, and for enough money to live in luxury for the rest of his life.

That is a lifestyle business. Its only purpose is to fund the financial aspirations of the owner. There is no larger purpose, no overarching vision of something beyond his quality of life. I'll grant that his personal ambition extends beyond his current, very comfortable existence. But it only extends to a *more* comfortable existence. That is a matter of degree, not direction.

Legacy owners' principal motivation for exit is to secure the company as a vehicle for accomplishing something larger than their personal quality of life. By that definition there are probably legacy businesses that don't provide a luxurious lifestyle, but they satisfy the owner's desired level of creature comforts and support for that bigger vision. Perhaps something that allows an owner to go on missions to Africa twice each year might qualify.

When coaching, the Lifestyle owner is primarily concerned about personal proceeds. The Legacy owner is focused on continuation, although the thing to be continued might not be the company. The difference between the two doesn't necessarily dictate an exit strategy, but it does influence how it will be implemented.

> *Family or Employee Succession*: Both types of owners may want their children to inherit, or employees to purchase the business. The Lifestyle owner seeks a strategy that will maintain a supporting income through retirement. Frequently, that could require limited cash flow to the buyers for an extended period following transfer.
>
> The Legacy owner is more concerned with the next ownership generation's ability to take care of the generations to follow. They are more focused on the training and education of the successors, and whether they represent the owner's and the company's values.

Third Party Sales: Lifestyle owners are frequently seeking the largest payout possible. They are more likely to engage in value enhancement work, even at the expense of postponing a retirement date.

Legacy owners are far more concerned with *who* than *how much*. They seek a buyer who will retain employees, stay in the same location or support the same causes. There may be customers who receive special treatment as underutilized or non-profit enterprises. Price is usually a secondary issue, even if the legacy considerations mean accepting less than full market value for the business.

Coaching the Lifestyle owner is relatively straightforward. He or she typically prioritizes proceeds. Their target may be in reach currently, or it may require some value enhancement work. Either way, the coaching aspect will focus on those features or changes that will provide the best bang for the buck.

> The Lifestyle owner is primarily concerned about personal proceeds.

An effective way to coach a Lifestyle owner when considering their timeframe, is to walk him or her through an initial due diligence list. When they see how many things can affect the multiple, their timeframe might be extended to deal with the value killers. The alternative is probably to scale back the anticipated proceeds.

The Legacy owner usually understands that an internal transfer to family or employees isn't the best route to maximize proceeds. Usually, those transfers require some compromises on valuation. The Legacy owner is less likely to be attracted to an auction-type environment. The concept of a company as the vehicle for legacy goals is quickly tarnished with the realization that a new owner has no obligations to maintain *anything* that the previous owner did.

Every owner, every company and every situation is unique. There are Lifestyle owners who have made enough money to satisfy their needs and are only interested in getting out. They may be willing to accept a substantial discount in return for more time to enjoy their retirement.

Conversely, there are Legacy owners whose objectives involve cash investment in a cause that isn't served directly by the company, and maximizing the value of the business is more important than maintaining its culture or current workforce.

Like the concept of "rich," the determination of whether an owner is more motivated by lifestyle or legacy is a critical part of your coaching connection as a trusted advisor.

THE COACHING DISCOVERY PROCESS

Coaching discovery as a process is the skill of seeing everything through the owner's eyes. In order to do that well, advisors should keep in mind the key factors when coaching business owners.

They are different from other business people. They live in a world where the outcome of their decisions is more personal, both emotionally and materially.

They are accustomed to making all of the important decisions. The best way to get their buy in is to give them control. You can point out the strengths and weaknesses of their choices, but in the end the decision is theirs. Any attempt to drive a specific strategy against their wishes is doomed to failure.

Coaching is a defined and chosen role. Both the client and the other advisors should be informed of your position as the coach, and accept it. As an advisor, you are taking the responsibility of helping the owner understand options and choose between them.

Coaching is about your questions. This requires more listening than speaking, and more questions than answers. Ask, then examine the answers and ask more. If you aren't sure of the objectives, if you aren't confident in the accuracy of the answer, or if you think there is more to it than what you know now, keep asking.

Understand the most important objective. It isn't a dollar amount or a timeframe. It's Lifestyle or Legacy.

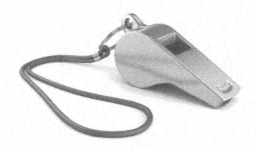

PART TWO: COACHING DISCOVERY
THE APPROACH

Many industries use the term "most trusted advisor." Besides the claim, they do little to define what achieving that status requires. Here is a news flash. It doesn't come from giving good advice.

The most trusted advisor is the one the business owner calls first, even when they know that the question or issue is outside the advisor's expertise. The most trusted advisor is there for a pulse check, direction, feedback and as the gateway to other advisors.

You become the most trusted advisor by genuinely demonstrating an interest in the client and their goals. You do that by asking questions and listening. Having deeper conversations about an owner's history, knowledge, desires and objectives is the purpose of coaching. It is the skill of helping a client reach conclusions based on those factors, not telling him what you think he should do.

The **approach** of coaching discovery uses the words like a compound noun. Coaching as a noun is defined by the Cambridge Dictionary as "The act of giving special classes in…a work-related activity, especially to one person." This is the focus of Part Two - the technique of coaching business owners.

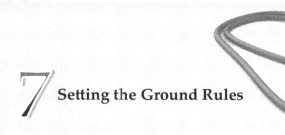

7 Setting the Ground Rules

"You don't get much done if you only work on the days you feel like it."

~ Jerry West

The Up Front Contract

Entering into any business relationship requires agreement by both sides regarding expectations and results. For complex or highly technical relationships, that may involve a written contract. For the vast majority of business dealings however, contracts are verbal, and any expectation of future performance is based on trust.

> Entering into any business relationship requires agreement by both sides regarding expectations and results.

When an advisor chooses a coaching role, he or she may be venturing outside of their normal comfort zone. It may also be outside the client's expectations of the role (tax advisor, wealth manager) that has characterized the relationship up to this point. Both issues are best addressed by a verbal contract.

My verbal "Up Front Contract" goes something like this.

> *"You are engaging me to help you with your exit planning. In order to successfully address your objectives, I need to take on the role of a coach to you in your role as the quarterback of the process. All decisions will remain in your hands, but I am responsible for the quality of the outcome. That means that we will capitalize on the strengths of your goals but I may have to point out weaknesses and hold you to the timelines we've agreed on. I may also ask for your support if the other advisors on the team (who all work for you), aren't delivering what we asked or are delaying our progress. Is all that acceptable to you?"*

This takes about 30 seconds, but of course I don't just rattle it off and ask the client to agree. These are the points I make in our first meeting after engagement. I haven't had a client object, but if one did I would gladly refund any retainer and part ways. It would be far less painful than working with someone who pushes back on our process from the very beginning. In those cases things won't get better as we go along.

Here are some bullet points to help you define a coaching relationship.

- Speak the truth always, even when the client doesn't like it.
- Act as a fiduciary, putting the client's needs first.
- Track the progress of the client's work, as well as that of other advisors.
- Offer options, even when the client is certain his or her idea is the right one.
- Respect the work of other advisors, and solicit their input.
- Act as the defender of the client's objectives.
- Deliver your work on time, but respect the client's need to attend to business first.

Conducting the Orchestra

Another metaphor I use with clients is that of the coach as the conductor of an orchestra.

The conductor is unlikely to play any instrument well enough to qualify as a musician in the symphony. But their position is undeniably one of the most important to the entire symphonic team. Without someone keeping time and focusing on the contributions of the individual players, the music is unlikely to sound as good.

The exit planning coach is required to know how the music is supposed to sound. The "music" represents the objectives of the business owner. Understanding how it is supposed to "sound" requires a broad background in tax strategies, legal documentation, business operations, estate planning and finance. Like conductors, exit planning coaches may have areas where they are skilled, but they aren't as accomplished in the broad range of disciplines as the other specialists on the team.

> A great exit plan is the *Ninth Symphony* of advisory services.

I love all kinds of music, but there are few pieces that bring tears to my eyes. A quality symphony orchestra performing Beethoven's *Ninth Symphony* is one of them. For me, a great exit plan, built around the owner's clearly defined life objectives and executed by a team of cooperative professionals, is the *Ninth Symphony* of advisory services.

8. Speaking the Truth

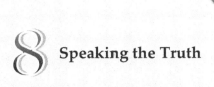

"Average players want to be left alone. Good players want to be coached. Great players want to be told the truth."

~ Doc Rivers

Digging Out the "Little Lie"

As I said in Chapter 6, a coach is a truth-sayer. It isn't always comfortable, but discomfort is a poor reason for violating your contract with the client. Telling the truth *should* be uncomfortable, especially if the other party is a business owner who is being less than truthful with you or, just as likely, with himself.

> Telling the truth *should* be uncomfortable.

I don't mean that a client is lying to you (although that sometimes happens as well). The most often told "lie" is one they believe themselves. Here is one that is popular as I write this.

"COVID really put a stranglehold on our business. We are still struggling to recover."

Yes, more than a hundred thousand restaurants went out of business. The entire hospitality industry, and service industries in general, were badly hurt. Office furniture dealers, real estate agents, in-home services and personal grooming businesses got hammered.

Following that, the American economy rebounded at the fastest rate in the last 40 years. It touched off an inflationary spiral that created a whole new set of problems.

But you aren't talking with a restaurant owner. The person on the other side of the table owns a manufacturing company, a wholesale business, or a construction company. Most of those, in my experience, were enjoying record or near-record years following COVID.

Yet most advisors will avoid the obvious. Sometimes it's because they want to appear empathetic. Perhaps they are still trying to win the prospect as a client. But too often their answer is something like "Yes I know. The pandemic has been hard on a lot of companies."

Deep down, the owner knows that competitors in his industry or market are thriving. He or she is making an excuse that they know (or at least suspect) isn't true. And the advisor just *bought* it! How smart does that make the advisor appear? When the owner is making an excuse that is unsupportable, it's the coach's duty to go deeper.

I respond in a supportive way, but without buying into the owner's excuse. "Yes, the pandemic hurt a lot of companies, but most that I know in your industry have recovered quite nicely. Have you considered that perhaps your business is lagging behind for some other reason?"

Remember, the strongest argument in any conversation is "I totally agree with you, *but…*"

Of course, I have to be confident that I am on solid ground. There may very well be another reason. For example, a paper goods supplier who specialized in serving small restaurants may have good reason to be lagging behind. That would be a reason for the slow recovery, but it also points out another issue. The business is too dependent on one type of customer, and needs to diversify its markets. Without questioning the initial statement, the advisor would not have that information.

I had the "It's the Great Recession, you know." given to me as a reason for declining sales in 2018! For those with short memories, the Great Recession ended in 2009. Sometimes an owner starts with a valid reason, and it just becomes an automatic knee-jerk excuse. It's the coach's job to haul that "little lie" into the light. If you don't, buying into the "little lie" serves your client poorly.

> The strongest argument in any conversation is, "I totally agree with you, but…"

Challenging Beliefs

There is a time to call out the client's easy excuse, and a time to recognize when someone really, really believes that he is speaking a truth.

That doesn't mean you have to roll over when an argument is forcefully made. You just need to be a bit more tactful in your challenges.

When I interview owners, I often ask why I would do business with their company over their competitors. The answers are often so standard that I could recite them before the owner does.

"We are good at what we do. We charge a fair price – not the cheapest in the industry, but not the most expensive either. If we make a mistake, we do whatever is necessary to make it right."

My response is also pretty standard. "So if I search for your business on the web, how many competitors will I find claiming to be incompetent price gougers who leave their customers high and dry if there is a problem?"

"No one would say that!"

"Then I return to my original question. Why would I do business with you?"

"Because we give great customer service!"

Whatever is the percentage of advisors who will challenge a client's first-level statement, only a small fraction of those will challenge a second time. Here is my response to that very standard claim of service differentiation.

"In *Competitive Strategy*, Michel Porter said there were two strategies, low cost and differentiation. The latter requires spending money. How much do you invest in differentiating your customer service?"

> I don't tell the client that he is wrong, I merely ask for clarification.

Note that I don't tell the client that he is wrong, I merely ask for clarification. He isn't telling the "little lie," but rather expressing his true belief. It's only when he has to back up his belief with evidence that he begins to check his premises.

Sometimes you have to walk a fine line. There is no benefit in confronting a client. You can't call them a liar or accuse them of being stupid. On the other hand, you can't just go along with everything they say.

When the quarterback says, "The receivers were all covered!" the coach doesn't say, "No they weren't. Jones and Murphy were both wide open!" He says instead "We'll have to go over the game film and see how they planned that coverage." He knows that when they get into the film room, the quarterback will be the first to notice his open teammates.

The coach doesn't challenge him in the middle of the game. He just helps the quarterback see for himself.

The Most Sensitive Subject
I recently had a conversation about coaching business owners with an attorney colleague. We were discussing how often owners have an inflated impression of their company's market value.

It's easy to understand. A business owner is totally vested in his or her company. By "totally" I mean mentally, physically, and emotionally tied to the success of the business as a measurement of their personal value as a human being. In the words of Ted Turner, "Life is a game. Money is how we keep score."

I'm not going to argue whether that *should* be the measure of success. Let's just accept for the moment that for a lot of folks, it is. If money is the scoring mechanism, a higher value for the business means that the owner is smarter, harder working, or better at whatever other criteria the "score" is supposed to indicate. It's not surprising that owners latch on to the highest value they can justify. Like many things, after they tell it to a few people it becomes "fact" in their minds.

We will talk specifically about coaching around impressions of valuation in Part Three, but for now, let's just take a typical response to "How do you know what your company is worth?"

> *"I talked to a guy at our industry trade show, and he knew a guy in another state who had a business a lot like mine. He said it sold for five million. I think my business is bigger than that one, so it's worth at least six or seven million."*

He told his financial planner that his business was worth $6,000,000, and the planner dutifully entered that as part of his retirement assumptions. He put that number on his personal income statement for a bank loan, and they didn't object because the bank was getting the owner's personal guarantee anyway.

So having been floated past two "financial experts," the value has become fact.

Mistaken impressions about value aren't the little lie, nor are they (usually) a firmly held belief. They are just a mistake. Unfortunately, they are a mistake that has a lot of ego attached. I approach it by calling the source into question rather than challenging the owner's number directly.

It requires some examination of the process that led him to his belief.

"Have you used this value for any other purposes?"

"Yes, I gave it to my financial planner, and to my banker when he approved my new line of credit."

"Did your financial planner confirm it with another source, or is he assuming that you know what your value is?"

"I guess he figures that it is my business, so I would have a pretty good idea of its value."

"How about the banker. Did he ask for a personal guarantee, or did he approve the loan based on your company value?"

"Well, I did have to sign a personal guarantee."

"So both sources are taking your word for it, without any objective support?"

"I guess so."

I'm not attacking what the client said, I'm just asking for more evidence. The conversation is abbreviated here. It doesn't really come across as a cross-examination, of course. My purpose in questioning isn't to "win" the point. It is to have the client consider the fact that he might want to get another opinion of his company's value from a more qualified source.

> You aren't attacking what the client said, you're just asking for more evidence.

A side note here. I've asked scores of financial planners how many of their business owner clients list their company value as 50% or more of their net worth. Virtually 100% will agree that it is common. I then ask how many have validated that number. Less than 10% have. Their usual answer is the one I used above. "He owns the business. I'm sure he knows what it is worth."

I'm not a financial planner, but I would be concerned if 50% or more of my client's retirement assumptions were based on something he overheard at a trade show. Just sayin'.

The same can be said about other assumptions an owner makes. Perhaps her employees have told her how talented her son is, and she has expanded the compliments to a belief that he has the qualifications to take over as CEO. The fact that the employees like him is only a very small part of what the job entails.

Similar assumptions can arise about financial ratios and profitability.

One client of mine had a successful roofing company. Revenues were in the middle eight figures, and he had built it up from his father's founding of it 35 years before. They had over 200 employees, and worked locally as well as on specific commercial applications around the nation..

Not surprisingly, he was approached by a private equity group that was rolling up roofing companies. After due diligence, he decided not to move forward with the transaction. He did learn something though.

> *"In the due diligence process, we were able to review the financial statements of their previous acquisitions. As a second generation roofer, I <u>knew</u> that companies like ours had to work hard to generate a 4% bottom line. Some years were a little better, and some much worse, but if you were hitting 4% regularly you were running a pretty good roofing business.*
>
> *I was stunned to discover that they were purchasing roofing companies with 7% and 8% pre-tax profits. A few had profits as high as 12%! We had no idea that you could make that kind of money in roofing!"*

As I said, he decided not to sell to the roll-up. He did, however, set out to at least double his margins. I'm happy to say that he succeeded. He just didn't know it could be done.

Distinguishing Knowing and Not Knowing

There are little lies. There are mistaken beliefs. There are "everybody knows" assumptions. Any or all of them might be false, or it just might be a case of you don't know what you don't know.

This becomes a problem when you are helping someone plan for the biggest financial transaction of their lives. If the client's baseline information is way off, everything that follows is corrupted.

> **If the client's baseline information is way off, everything else that follows is corrupted.**

One of our commonly used tag lines for the ExitMap® is "Asking the right questions, in the right order." There are some questions that a client expects and anticipates. Everyone asks them. "What do you want to have happen with your business?" "How much do you think your business is worth?" "When do you want to retire?"

The job of the coach is to ask the questions that the client doesn't anticipate, and then validate the answers.

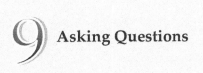 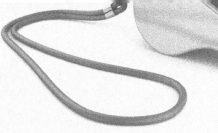

Asking Questions

"The one who knows all the answers has not been asked all the questions."
~ Confucius

There are questions, and there are questions. Using questions correctly can create a bond with a client. Using them incorrectly can make you seem nosy and intrusive.

Start With an Observation
Beginning a question with an observation, especially a complimentary observation, puts clients at ease. They know why you are asking, and have an opportunity to frame the answer. Even the few seconds of stating your observation gives them time to mentally move to the right space. Just asking the question outright may make some uncomfortable, since any pause in their answer feels like they are displaying a lack of knowledge or a lack of confidence.

Here are a few examples:

Instead of "Describe your company culture to me," try "I see that your employees seem pretty happy. What do you do to help create that attitude?"

Instead of "What percentage of your business comes from your top five customers?" You could use "Many companies in your industry depend on a few big customers for a large portion of their sales. Is that the case with you?"

Instead of "What operational decisions do you delegate?" You could say "I notice that we aren't interrupted while we are meeting. Is someone else handling routine decisions while we are together, or will you have employees waiting for you as soon as we are done?"

61

Questions that are easier to answer, even if you sacrifice a bit of specificity in the answers, make the client more comfortable. That's a big step in creating the most trusted advisor relationship.

> Too many advisors fall into the trap of asking yes/no questions.

Open Ended Questions

Too many advisors fall into the trap of asking yes/no questions. "Do you know the value of your business?" is worse than asking no question at all. If the business owner says "No," the coach is backed into answering the question for him. You can't move on to the next question, because the "No" answer begs for a solution. No matter what the coach's next comment is, it is the advisor talking instead of the client.

If the owner's answer is "Yes," the coach has no more information than he had before asking the question. How does the owner know? Where did he get the information? Is the source reliable? Are his calculations reliable? No matter what the follow-on answers are, the first yes/no question was a waste of time.

Every coach has to practice open-ended questioning. At the outset of any interview, these questions should start a business owner on the road to more fully describing their business and personal goals.

- How did you get your start in this business?
- What did you do before you owned this company?
- What does your ideal customer look like?
- How do you decide to add a new product or service?
- Who are your top 3 employees, and why did you choose them?
- What is your timeline for transitioning from this business, and why did you choose it?
- What are your toughest challenges?

- How do you define success?
- What do you see as the biggest challenge to your transition?
- If you bought this company, what would you do to grow the business?
- Where do new customers come from?
- What are your weaknesses as a business owner?

Coaches should practice making questions open-ended. Whether you use these questions or others, I recommend writing down your "best" open-ended questions and keeping them in front of you during the discussion.

Not: "Do you offer terms on your sales?" but rather, "How quickly do your customers pay you?"

Not: "Can your employees make decisions without you?" Instead: "How does the company function when you aren't here?"

Not: "Is your marketing effective?" but "How do you track which marketing expenditures are the most effective?"

And the biggest open-ended exit planning question of all:

"What will you do when you no longer run this company?"

Using Forms

I am going to take a moment here to talk about the value of forms in coaching interviews.

I've used interview forms for about 25 years. At first I was reluctant, because I worried that prospective clients would regard my questioning as too formulaic. Fortunately, my laziness and selfishness took over.

Too often I would review my notes and realize that I had forgotten to ask a key question. Without the answer, my proposals would be light in areas I wanted to mention or focus on. I could call the client and say "I forgot to ask you something." That didn't reflect well on my professionalism. Alternatively, I could fake it. I write well enough that it wasn't obvious, but I knew in my next meeting I would have to go back and cover that ground again. That was selfish. I was only trying to maintain my image of expertise.

Even when I remembered to ask the question, I would often have to go back to my notes saying "Where did he answer that?" I may have written the answer down, or perhaps not. What if I didn't and misremembered the answer? That was my laziness, and was remedied by having the client's answers organized in a way that I could easily find them on my form.

As I moved from consulting into more of a coaching role, I learned to use an interview form developed by David Halpern, the former owner of the Merry-Go-Round chain of boutiques and one of my mentors. It flowed logically from an up front contract ("Do we agree on why we are meeting?") to exploration through open ended questions, to identification of the prospect's issues, to a summary focused on closing the sale.

As the years went on, I added some hints in the closing section based on my study of and subsequent certification in, behavioral profiling. It was amazingly effective, and the process has been successful in closing roughly 500 advisory engagements with business owners.

A qualifying note: In my peer group coaching business I employed up to 8 contracted coaches at any given time. I didn't *deliver* all those services to 500 owners by myself! It is more challenging to sell the expertise of someone who isn't in the room with you. It requires that the prospect trust you enough at the end of the interview to accept your recommendation that someone whom they haven't met can provide the solution to their problem. Organizing the interview in a form helped assure that I didn't wander off into trying to impress them with my personal expertise. That would have been counterproductive to my objectives.

We include such structured interview forms in the ExitMap® toolkit, but if you aren't a subscriber, you can certainly create some on your own. The key is to make sure that they are comprehensive and that you feel comfortable using them in a meeting.

As I start an introductory meeting with a prospect, I take out the interview form. I say "It's important to me that I am able to refer back to what you tell me about your business. I want to respect your time, and make certain that I ask all the pertinent questions. I hope you don't mind if I use this form to better organize our discussion and make notes."

> "I hope you don't mind if I use this form to better organize our discussion and make notes."

I have *never* had anyone object. Who would protest that what they say isn't worth recording, that their time isn't valuable, or that they don't think you should be organized? It sets the tone for the whole meeting. The fact that you are writing down what they say also tends to make them more conscious of giving complete, detailed responses.

Forms have another advantage. I include the key factors that improve success rates in closing an engagement so that I have a reminder when the time comes. I'll discuss this more in the chapter on behavioral profiling.

1.0 Listening

"And so I had him thinking of me as a good conversationalist when, in reality, I had been merely a good listener and had encouraged him to talk."

~ Dale Carnegie

One Mouth, Two Ears

You've heard it since you were a child. Although coaching may be about asking questions, *successful* coaching requires that you listen to the answers.

The more you listen to someone, the smarter they think you are. Beginning your first meeting by letting the prospective client talk as much as possible isn't just an ego boost for the client. It says that you are really interested in what they have to say.

> Most advisors are looking for the opportunity to show how smart they are.

Listening is a difficult skill for most advisors. After all, we get paid for our opinions. Sitting silently while someone else goes on about their business (or themselves) is contrary to our trained professional behavior. Most advisors are looking for the opportunity to show how smart they are, and many clients give them that opportunity every minute and a half or so.

Try this exercise. List five short statements that are relatively generic, like, "Tell me about your business," or "Describe your best employee." See if you can get through a five-minute conversation saying nothing but those statements. With normal speech patterns, that would mean the other person should say about 600 words for your 40 or so.

Even though the "You were given two ears and one mouth" aphorism indicates a 2:1 ratio, the more you let a prospective client speak at the outset of your conversation, the more you will learn and the more trusting of you they will be. The 15 to 1 ratio in the exercise above is a little extreme, but it is good practice.

In order for the client's answers to be informative and impactful, the right questions have to be asked correctly, and in the right order.

In the previous chapter I discussed the value of using forms. ExitMap® has forms for every information gathering meeting with the client. Our coaching tools have structured forms for an initial Assessment debriefing (where the advisor is trying to land an engagement), our Business Baseline initial discovery and our Personal Vision Builder. Each has places to write down notes and the client's responses.

Our Personal Vision Builder particularly is an interactive form used so that the client can see the effect of his or her responses on long term cash flow and retirement expectations, along with the impact on daily activities in life's "next act." Like the other two forms mentioned, it is intended to create a deeper conversation.

> Interview forms are intended to create deeper conversations.

I occasionally have an advisor call me and say "I filled in all the blanks and I still don't know what the client's exit plan should be." They have missed the point. A conversation, by definition, is not fill-in-the-blanks.

If, for example the client answers "Yes" when asked if he has discussed ownership with a key employee, checking off the "Yes" space isn't the purpose of the question. It should lead to additional questions like: Who broached the topic of ownership, was it you or was it the employee? What have you told them? Did you promise ownership in the future? Do you know if they expect to buy in, or to get their ownership as a gift?

That's why my interview forms end up with margin notes, underlines, stars and words that are circled. It's because I want to recall more than just the answer. I need to record what I *heard*.

Having the interview questions written out gives me a number of other advantages in these discussions. First, I don't forget questions. I suffer frequently from what the French call *"l'esprit de l'escalier"* or "the spirit of the stair." That's when you think of the right thing to say…just after you've walked out of the room!

They also give me an excuse to be quiet while I am recording responses, and it frees me up to *listen*. When you are interviewing, it's very easy to focus on what you are going to ask next. Inevitably, that means you are listening less, and listening less is no way to become trusted as an advisor.

Sounds of Silence

Let's take the art of listening one step further. How comfortable are you with silence?

When I am interviewing any prospect or client, I always take notes. Even when using interview forms, I'm not just filling in their answers. I am annotating the responses. ("Very excited," or "Really doesn't like this.") One reason is to have something I can refer to later, but that is the least important. Taking notes serves three other purposes.

1. It shows that I think what the interviewee is saying is important to me.

2. Since I am both listening and writing, I get the benefit of double learning and am less likely to forget what the client said.

3. It gives me an excuse <u>not</u> to talk.

I'll ask an open-ended question. Let's take the first one from the list above. "How did you get your start in this business?"

The client answers "I was brought up in it. My father founded the company."

A perfectly good answer, but the client does not continue to talk, and I don't have enough information. So I'll busy myself writing notes (I typically use a handwriting application on my tablet computer.) Usually between 5 and 10 seconds will do it. That's long enough for most clients to become uncomfortable with the silence.

"I started at the bottom. I had to do every menial job in the business before my Dad would let me work in the office."

Still no response from me. If it goes uncomfortably long (over ten seconds) I may make a continuation comment, perhaps "Uh huh?" just to make it plain that I don't plan to jump in here.

"Once I got a desk job, he tried to have me keep the books, but I really didn't like it."

"No?"

"No, accounting is boring. I like talking to customers much better."

Still no comment.

"I became pretty good at sales, and within a year was the top salesperson in the company."

The entire exchange only took two or three minutes, but by being quiet I now know the client's strengths and weaknesses, his father's approach to training him, and the likely area where he focuses his energies.

I learned a lot more than merely the fact that he's worked in the company for his whole career. He isn't just the son of the boss; he earned his spurs with sales ability. I also know to check his financial records carefully. Since they bore him, there is a good chance he isn't watching the numbers as carefully as someone else might.

> By being quiet you now know the client's strengths and weaknesses.

He began with a short (11-word) response to my 9-word question. From there, silence and 3 continuation syllables extended his answer by another 71 words. Quite a substantial return merely for just keeping my mouth shut for a couple of extra seconds. That's 82 words from him in response to 12 words from me. That's almost a seven to one ratio. Not bad!

11 Coaching about Value

"It is difficult, but not impossible, to conduct strictly honest business."

~ Mahatma Gandhi

The Valuation Obstacle

The Pepperdine Private Capital Markets Survey canvasses intermediaries who sell privately held Main Street and mid-market companies. (See the afterward for a discussion of defining those terms.) When asked about obstacles that prevented the sale of a business, the number one response is "Owner's unreasonable expectations of value."

Recently, I asked a business owner what he thought his company was worth. Here is (almost verbatim) his response:

> "A friendly competitor in my city sold his business last year. He had about a dozen employees, I have three. He owned all of his equipment, I rent mine as needed. He also owned the building his business operated from, which was on two acres of land. We work from my house.
>
> I know he sold the business along with the equipment and real estate for a million dollars, so I think mine is probably worth about $800,000."

Sometimes it is difficult not to look incredulous when a statement like that is made, but owners believe what they want to believe.

Valuation is a sensitive subject. Some owners feel that because they worked in the business for thirty or forty years, it would be only fair that it fund their next twenty years in retirement. Their target price is set only by their desired lifestyle after the business.

> **Some owners target a price set only by their desired lifestyle after the business.**

Others look at the Price-to-Earnings ratios of publicly traded firms in their industry, and assume the same multiples will apply to their business. At the beginning of 2022, the PE (price to earnings) ratio of the Dow Jones Industrial Average was 32. The only private companies that sell for that kind of multiple are earlier-stage tech plays where venture capitalists measure expected future growth in orders of magnitude. The typical Baby Boomer owner does not own such a business.

Still others have a general idea of the multiples paid in their industry, but try to use multiples of Seller's Discretionary Earnings (SDE) and apply them to EBITDA-based pricing models.

As I mentioned earlier, most say something like this:

> "I talked to a guy at our industry trade show, and he knew a guy in another state who had a business a lot like mine. He said it sold for six ex, or about five million. I think my business is bigger than that one, so it has to be worth at least six or seven million."

Besides basing a valuation on hearsay, this statement has lots of other issues. Obviously, he doesn't know much about the other business. It could be more profitable. It may have some strategic differentiation or other feature that made it unique. He is quoting a multiple without understanding what is being multiplied, and a price without knowing the breakdown of components.

Another problem is the fact that many sellers are lying, or to be more forgiving, quoting the highest number they can possibly justify without plainly lying. Not to disparage them, but as I said previously, the longer they believe the lie, the sooner it becomes their truth.

Sellers "Lie"

I put "lie" in quotation marks because most sellers of a small business don't do it intentionally. They aren't valuation professionals, and everyone wants to make their transaction appear as important and lucrative as they can. As a result, owners frequently foster the impression that their business is worth more than it actually is.

Here is an example. The former owner is asked how much his business sold for. He responds, "Just a bit short of six million dollars." It sounds pretty good, right? But if we could see the closing documents, this is how it could break down for an asset sale by an owner in the 35% income tax bracket.

PURCHASE	PRICE	TAXES	EXPLANATION	NET PROCEEDS TO SELLER
Property, Plant and Equipment	$2,500,000	$965,000	The assets were fully depreciated, with depreciation recovery at ordinary income tax plus Obamacare premium (38.6%).	$1,535,000
Accounts receivable	$800,000	N/A	Dollar for dollar purchase of the proceeds from business done prior to the transaction. This was the seller's money anyway.	0
Line of Credit	$350,000	N/A	Retirement of debt incurred by the seller. He received this money from the bank previously.	0
Leases	$150,000	N/A	Payoff on leases owed by seller.	0
Cash left in the bank as working capital	($300,000)	N/A	Tangible net equity left as part of the purchase agreement, essentially a reduction of the purchase price.	($300,000)
Earn Out	$1,200,000	TBD if paid	*Maximum* contingent payment for reaching future growth targets.	TBD
2 year consulting agreement	$450,000		Requires continued employment - not really part of the sale price.	
Escrow	$500,000		Contingent payment after post-closing due diligence.	TBD
Total	$5,950,000	Owner's Sale Price	Net proceeds at close	$1,235,000

So in reality, "Almost $6,000,000" breaks down into $1,235,000 in the owner's pocket, about $1,042,800 (post-tax) in *possible* future payments, and a job for two years. Perhaps that is a totally acceptable result for the owner, but it is a whole lot less than the "just a bit short of $6,000,000" that he claims.

From his perspective the owner isn't lying, but anyone not in possession of the transaction documents would be hard put to figure out the difference.

Valuations are Confusing

Helping a client reach a good understanding of his or her business's value is a critical component of exit coaching. It is the underpinning of any retirement planning. It drives any sales negotiation or internal succession structure.

> Being able to win a client's agreement to something that differs from their expectations is a key factor in your acceptance as the most trusted advisor.

Most importantly, being able to win a client's agreement to something that differs from their expectations is a key factor in your acceptance as the most trusted advisor.

I recently worked with a client who, in responding to our initial Assessment questionnaire, said, "I have a certified appraisal of my business." When I looked at the appraisal, it showed a value of nearly five million dollars.

Since this client wanted to explore a sale to a key employee, the cash flow available to fund such a transfer was critical. When I looked at the appraisal, however, a value had been assigned that was over twenty times the annual cash flow. At that rate, the key employee would be paying for the purchase over several decades.

With the client's permission, I contacted the appraiser. He explained that the valuation was the result of several factors.

- It was done for the purpose of an IRS examination of the estate. (The father/founder had recently passed away.) As such it required inclusion of all the assets in the company, and certain other calculations, whether they were material to the business operations or not.

- The assets that were included were:
    - Excess working capital (cash accounts not needed for daily operations) of over $1,500,000
    - About $300,000 in the stock of a mutual company, which for some reason was owned by the business
    - Life insurance with a cash surrender value of over $750,000

Once we backed out these non-business assets, the enterprise value of the company was less than half what the valuation showed. It took some considerable explaining, but the owner finally understood why his presumed windfall in the value of the business wasn't sustainable. Of course, in this case it was helped by the realization that there was some 2.5 million dollars in value that was available to him without selling the company.

What is a "Certified" Valuation?

The term "Certified Valuation" is confusing. It broadly means that the appraisal was done by a professional with a recognized certification for this type of work. It should be done according to AICPA and, if appropriate, Internal Revenue Service standards. Unless such use is declaimed in the summary letter, it should be acceptable in legal proceedings as a fair value for the company.

There is one problem.

A fair value for the company, developed according to appraisal standards, may be very different from the Fair Market Value (FMV).

Here is another example.

A client asked a CPA firm to appraise her business. A 5-office medical services firm organized as a C corporation, she had dutifully drawn down almost all the profits every year as bonuses, on the advice of her tax attorney. She expensed as many things as she could as business write offs, including her car, home office and considerable travel.

The appraising CPA firm (not her tax firm) found little in the way of historical earnings. There were few assets other than some desks and chairs, and few examples in the way of comparative sales. The appraiser dutifully priced the business at the value of the assets, which was about $200,000.

Two months later she sold the business for $2,000,000.

Why was the difference so great? A "Certified" valuation must use one or more of three methods specified by the Appraisal Standards Board (ASB).

1. **Asset value.** In this case, some partially depreciated furniture in leased offices was the only tangible asset.

2. **Income** from future cash flows. This is where some intermediaries who conduct "valuation" seminars in hotel ballrooms develop big numbers. They tell the attendees to take their current cash flow, multiply it by a growth rate (usually 10% to 15% annually) and extend it out 12 years or so. Then they calculate the Net Present Value of all those earnings. There is only one problem. Except in venture capital investments, no buyer intends to pay *you* for the growth of the business under *their* ownership.

3. **Market Comparatives.** There are several places to look for sales of similar businesses. For very small businesses, Tom West publishes the *Business Reference Guide* with "Rules of Thumb" for many Mom and Pop businesses. DealStats is a database of Main Street business sales. While helpful, much of the information is dated and it requires a lot of judgement to weed out transactions that just don't "look" right. There is no check that I know of

on the accuracy of submissions. Another source is to look up the value of publicly traded companies. As mentioned earlier, those have no relation to smaller business's valuations.

So, in the absence of earnings to develop an NPV (Net Present Value), and lacking a reasonable source of comparative sales, the CPA chose Assets as the only source of confirmable information for his certified valuation. The company's dominance in the market, and its contracts with local insurance companies weren't part of his consideration.

What is the "Right" Price?

The owner's objective for the proceeds of a transition has a big influence on his or her exit plan. The "right price" is usually some combination of what the owner expects and what the market will bear.

In the final analysis, price is always a function of cash flow. A more desirable company can get a higher multiple of cash flow, but every deal is based on the expected return.

A buyer who can pay cash for a company is a rare find, but even then, the price will be dependent on the buyer's expectations for a return on investment or ROI. Most sellers don't realize it, but any multiple of cash flow is predicated on the ROI, and therefore sets the price.

A buyer who expects a 20% ROI will pay a multiple of five times cash flow. One who expects 25% will pay a multiple of four, etc. That is why a professional buyer, such as a private equity fund, may pay more than an individual buyer. A multiple of 6.25 times cash flow yields an ROI of 16% annually. More than six years may seem like a long payback for an investment, but a fund that returns 16% annually (before expenses) would be very attractive to most investors.

Pointing this out to a business owner goes a long way towards helping them understand the dynamics of the marketplace. Yes, a more substantial buyer will usually pay more, but there are lots of other issues such as minimum cash flow, quality of earnings audits and tangible net equity requirements.

This approach makes any variation in the way cash value calculations are done pretty impactful. Professional acquirers such as private equity groups and publicly traded companies measure cash flow as Earnings Before Interest (a financing decision not relevant to post transaction cash flow), Taxes, Depreciation and Amortization (two non-cash deductions from earnings for tax purposes).

In Main Street companies, where the buyer expects to operate the business as a source of livelihood, cash flow is usually measured as "Sellers Discretionary Earnings" or SDE. If EBITDA is a measure of Return on Investment, SDE is a measure of Return on Labor. It includes other benefits such as health insurance, retirement contributions, automobile expenses, and travel for industry conferences or continuing education.

Another client was discussing the potential for a sale with an investment bank. The price they recommended was far below his target. When queried, they pointed to his recently completed tax return, which showed profits at about 80% lower than his internal statements had indicated.

The owner, like so many others, had breathed a sigh of relief when his tax accountant told him he had no need to make additional tax payments, and dutifully forwarded the return to the investment bank.

The "missing" millions were the result of converting the internal records (done on accrual) to cash basis for the IRS. It was legitimate and easily corrected, and the investment bank's suggested pricing rose proportionately.

> A valuation isn't always about fair market value.

These are just examples of why a valuation isn't always about fair market value. Your tax accountant usually seeks to reduce taxable earnings. Appraisals done for different purposes may use different approaches, and when the Internal Revenue Service is the intended recipient, the methods may differ from any other use. Finally, an appraiser is bound by certain rules that may not mimic the open market.

Fannie Mae defines Fair Market Value as

> *The most probable price that a property should bring in a competitive and open market under all conditions requisite to a fair sale, the buyer and seller, each acting prudently, knowledgeably and assuming the price is not affected by undue stimulus.*

It's up to the coach to help the client understand when a third-party valuation may or may not be suitable for exit planning, and determine what measurement the target buyers will be using.

A Coaching Approach to Value Discussions

Many advisors will challenge an owner on their valuation assumptions. Although I have already said that it's the coach's job to tell the truth, sometimes discretion is the better part of valor. Telling an owner flat out that you think their company is worth far less than they think, is usually one of those times.

Alternatively, some advisors will duck the value question by suggesting a third-party valuation. Although a good appraisal has excellent application in exit planning, getting one takes time, and we aren't looking for ways to slow our engagement down.

We use the ExitMap® Seller's Sanity Check© spreadsheet to help owners understand the practical issues of valuation. The spreadsheet has the requirements of the Small Business Administration (SBA) for lending guarantees. It includes minimum owner compensation, cash flow to debt service ratios and down payment, along with various financing structures for a third-party lender and subordinated financing.

We use the SBA parameters only because they are consistent nationwide. Different lenders have more or less stringent requirements, but the SBA requirements are a reasonable starting point.

We invite the owner to plug his or her assumed valuation into the spreadsheet along with our agreed-upon cash flow calculations, and then start "building the deal." They can project down payments along with financing by up to three lenders with rates and terms. The spreadsheet fills in a projected salary for the new owner (the SBA will not accept owner compensation below the rate that is determined by size of the purchase) and calculates the debt service ratio and down payment ROI.

The client can play with time frames, terms, interest rates, and (finally) the price until they have a "loan package" that a lender is likely to accept. I explain that this may not be the fair market value, but it is pretty close to how a lender will look at it. I call it "financeable value."

There may be a dozen other factors that would impact the fair market value of the company, but now we have a reasonably clear idea of how much the current cash flow will support. Then we can have a substantive conversation about what it would take to reach a different number.

> There may be a dozen other factors that would impact the fair market value of the company.

I don't have to confront the owner, nor do I tell them that they're wrong. I just help them discover *why* their pricing may be an issue. They are the ones who settle on an answer (which is far more acceptable than being told). I've helped them experiment and test their assumptions under real-life conditions. The conclusion is theirs, not mine. That's coaching.

It isn't the coach's role to understand all the vagaries of valuation. It is, however, important that you can understand that assigned values may be the results of anything from a casual conversation to a "certified" report costing thousands of dollars. The number may be greatly influenced by the source, timing or intended use of the information.

Valuation is an area where trust is paramount. The advisor frequently has to deal with inflated pricing expectations. As previously pointed out, in many cases the owner thinks that value has been "validated" by other professionals. However, you need to be the one the client believes for your relationship to be successful.

1.2 Behavioral Profiling

> *"I've found that every time I've gotten into trouble with a player, it was because I wasn't talking to him enough."*
> ~ Lou Holtz

Communicating Effectively

Part of the skill set of every successful coach is an ability to communicate. The coach understands that each player has differing listening skills. They process information individually. Some are more receptive to certain kinds of communication than others.

In our practice we use the DISC behavioral assessment. The basic theory of four types of behavior was developed by William Moulton Marston at Harvard in the 1930's. All behavioral measures use the four axes of behavior. If you've taken a Meyers Briggs, PF 16, or Predictive Index you are familiar with the four types. In DISC they are Dominance, Influence (originally Inducement), Steadiness (originally Submission), and Compliance. The terms were apparently changed because the 1930's characterizations of behavior aren't as well-received today.

I can't resist tossing in trivial knowledge. Not only was William Marston the father of behavioral profiling, he also invented an early version of the polygraph. In addition, he was a feminist, and a lifelong fan of Greek and Roman literature. He spent the last 7 years of his life (1941-1947) writing stories in DC Comics about a fictional character he had invented named Wonder Woman, an Amazonian daughter of a Greek god!

While a background in behavioral science is handy for any coach, most don't have the time or inclination to add that skill to their repertoire. There are a few simple hints that can be enormously helpful in tailoring your communication style to that of your client.

> The DISC approach gives excellent insights into how a person communicates.

The DISC approach doesn't indicate intelligence, ethics, or ability. It does, however, give excellent insight into how a person communicates, that is, how they receive and process information. We have been certified in one of the DISC tools (there are several) for many years, and use it with every client. It's tremendously valuable in knowing and understanding how to successfully approach an engagement.

Each behavioral style has two characteristics. Most people have two styles that are more prominent than the others, and this short guide only considers the most obvious, but even identifying only the most prominent is very effective.

Dominance is how you approach *problems*. A higher D tendency is someone who wants to overcome a problem. They perceive them as obstacles to their progress. A low D wants to circumnavigate problems. They are something to go around. The high D wants to solve things. The low D wants to find an alternative. As with every behavioral style, both the high and low measures of the train are legitimate approaches.

Influence is how you approach *people*. High I's talk to convey information and to get a listener to come around to their way of thinking. They believe that every issue can be addressed by talking it out. Low I's avoid conversation. They prefer to influence others with reports or articles. They can get very frustrated when a high I doesn't read their memos and says, "Just tell me about it." This is one of the most frequent breakdowns in team communication.

Steadiness is how you approach *process*. People who are high on the S scale could be characterized as those that "begin with the end in mind." They are great at preparing, but may be a bit slow to pull the trigger. A lower S will tend more towards "ready, fire, aim." Excellent strategists, the high S will usually go through all the "what if?" permutations of a plan before starting out.

Compliance behaviors are about *procedure*. Where process is internally generated, the high C is always looking for the rule book. They are risk averse and want to know who has done this before. The low C is epitomized by the classic line of the outlaws in John Huston's *Treasure of the Sierra Madre*, "Badges? We don't need no stinking badges!"

When Dominance or Influence styles are primary, the person tends to be extroverted.

When Steadiness or Compliance are primary, the person tends to be introverted.

When Dominance or Compliance are primary, the person tends to be focused on objective measurements or goals.

When Influence or Steadiness are primary, the person tends to be focused on people.

DOMINANCE HIGH D (Extrovert/Objects)	INFLUENCE HIGH I (Extrovert/People)	STEADINESS HIGH S (Introvert/People)	COMPLIANCE HIGH C (Introvert/Objects)
• Control of your future • Decision support • Defending your objectives	• Exiting options • Consideration of customers, vendors and employees	• Concern for culture • Information for good decisions • Continuity and security	• Carefully developed process • Risk mitigation • Concrete plans and options

Combining the two will help you identify the client's preferred communication style. Consciously accommodating that style will make your conversations more effective, engender greater cooperation and not incidentally, close more advisory engagements.

Recognizing Communication Styles

If the client directs the discussion, elucidates at length on conversational points, and changes topics frequently or easily, they are likely a D or an I. If the conversation and goals are concrete (an amount of money, a time frame, or acquisition of specific assets) they are a D. If the focus is on people (family security, employee retention, customer satisfaction) they are more likely an I.

If the client is taciturn or terse, answers questions sparingly and waits for you to lead every conversation, they are likely an S or a C. If the conversation revolves around people, they are probably an S. If it focuses on concrete benefits (especially if they are very involved in the detail) they are likely a C.

Millions of DISC assessments have been administered, and they are inordinately dependable. An advisor experienced in DISC can create an exercise and be almost certain of the outcome.

I was conducting an exercise for a national meeting of franchisees. I created a survival exercise in which they were on a company trip to Machu Picchu in Peru. Their tour bus had an accident, severely injuring their driver/guide. They had passed a village about 45 minutes before, say 30 miles down the mountain, and had not seen another vehicle on the road since. The guide had mentioned that another village was about 15 miles ahead.

Night was falling, they were above 6,000 feet and it was getting colder. There was no cellular service. What would you do?

I divided the group into 4 teams by their DISC profiles, and gave them 15 minutes to come up with a plan.

The first thing I heard was from someone in the High D group. *"I don't know what the rest of you are going to do, but this is what I'm going to do."* They never sat down, all standing for the 15 minutes in a circle with their arms folded. Some wanted to go for help, others wanted to wait. They decided to let each person individually decide what they wanted to do.

The High I group gathered closely around a table. They were having a terrific time, and their laughter drew the attention of everyone else several times over the next 15 minutes. When time was up, they were surprised. They had been having too much fun to actually discuss the problem.

The S group was amazing! (If you are ever in a similar crisis, stick with the S's.) They had pooled their snacks for rationing, stripped the vinyl covers off the bus seats to make shelters, used the aluminum tubing to splint the guide's injuries. (They were embellishing just a bit.) Finally, they had identified the most physically fit among them. One group would go down the mountain to seek help at the last village. A few in the best condition would hike uphill, hopefully to find help more quickly at the next village.

The C group decided to send a party down to the last village for help. Although they knew that the next village was supposed to be only one-third the distance, they hadn't been there yet. At least they knew what the road back down was like.

It works like that every time. I've done a number of these, and they always come out about the same.

> It's gratifying to have a client say, "You understand me better than my other advisors."

It sounds a little challenging, but if you listen to the client, especially how they respond to your open-ended questions, you will quickly learn to pick up on the two behavioral identifiers. It's gratifying to have a client say, "You understand me better than my other advisors."

Closing an Engagement

Remember, the objective of coaching is to become the client's *most* trusted advisor. That isn't something you stumble into. Cultivating that status is the result of conscious communication from the very first meeting.

We train our ExitMap® subscribers to read the behavioral clues (introverted or extroverted, discussing people or tangibles) when they are conducting an Assessment debriefing.

Our debriefings start with open ended questions to get the client talking. Asking about the business puts an owner on familiar ground and relaxes them. More importantly, I can pay attention to whether I am leading the conversation or they are (extrovert/introvert) and if the objectives are focused on people or objects.

I also like to throw in some gentle challenges or call a few of their answers into question. The D will refute it. The I will change it. The S will want to discuss approaches to a solution, and the C will ask for the source of your evidence or justification.

How can you utilize this? By tailoring your presentation in a way that the client thinks.

If they are a high D, describe the results that can be expected, how planning allows them to have control over their future, and how you, as a coach, will defend their objectives through the process.

If they are a high I, emphasize the number of options they have to choose from, and especially include the benefits to other stakeholders, people, customers, employees and family.

If they are a high S , show your concern for their company culture, the continuity and security that comes with a step-by-step process, and the importance of having sufficient information to make good decisions.

If they are a high C, emphasize that you use a carefully developed process in your approach, that it is proven with many other clients, and it reduces risk on the way to a concrete plan.

Be careful! You will see prospects who were wary, taciturn or standoffish turn around in a few minutes if you communicate in their style. You may feel that you are being manipulative, or that you have a secret agenda that preys on the client's ignorance. (Especially if you are a High I.)

Nothing could be further from the truth. Tailoring your communication style to your client's is so effective only because so few people do it. There is nothing underhanded about listening better and responding more clearly than most of your competition.

It's called good coaching. And by the way, it will probably double your closing rate for engagements.

13 Nobody Likes a Showoff

"Talent sets the floor, character sets the ceiling."
~ Bill Belichick

The Expertise Trap

When a prospect approaches you for advisory services, it can be difficult not to try and impress him. After all, you want him to think he is making a good decision in hiring you.

Leading with your expertise has some drawbacks.

It tempts the client to look for measurable confirmation. "I am the best at this." begs the response of "Exactly how good are you?" Once you've walked yourself down that path, "Very, very good." is seldom an acceptable answer. Unless you can give performance metrics, stay away from claiming greater expertise than the next guy.

You are also pigeonholing yourself. If you want to be the client's most trusted advisor, you want to be the first advisor they call, regardless of your area of greatest expertise. As a coach, your expertise lies in understanding your clients' needs. Saying they should hire you because of your tax advice or financial planning experience almost guarantees that they will assume a need to call someone else when their question is in another area.

> If you want to be the client's most trusted advisor, you want to be the *first* advisor they call.

Likewise, avoid jargon and acronyms as much as possible. Saying, "We frequently address that problem by creating an Intentionally Defective Grantor Trust, where the annuity payments fund ILIT premiums," helps 99% of your clients NOT AT ALL! It simply convinces them that they

87

won't understand what you are doing, can't be sure that you are doing it right, and can't explain it to anyone else.

In short, it makes them afraid of losing control. Remember, they are business owners because they *like* to be in control.

I recently received a call from one of our ExitMap® subscribers in another state. He wanted my opinion on a meeting he had just conducted with a client. The owners were two young men in their 30s who had built a rapidly growing technology company. They had recently received a venture capital investment that had valued the business at just under $100,000,000.

Excited by the idea of life-changing wealth, they wisely called a meeting of their advisors for the purpose of planning. The accounting firm invited a law firm that specialized in tax planning to sit in.

According to our colleague, who is a value enhancement business consultant, the lawyer listened to their story for a few minutes and then interrupted. "You clearly need a GRAT," the attorney said. "I will send you an illustration, and you can call us to get it started." He then said he had another meeting, and disconnected.

True to his word, the attorney emailed a PowerPoint slide illustrating a Grantor Retained Annuity Trust (GRAT) that would pay them at a rate of 51% interest annually, with their heirs receiving the stock at a much lowered basis.

I'm not a financial planner, but I haven't seen that kind of approach before for young owners who have no idea what their eventual outcome for the business, their lives and their families will look like. Perhaps my lack of expertise is showing, but it seemed another example of "To a hammer, everything is a nail."

For owners in their 30s, tying stock up in a trust can severely restrict their options in a sale. I also pointed out that the likelihood that their venture capital partners were prepared to let them walk away right after making a substantial equity investment was likely zero. Apparently, no one had brought up those issues in the meeting.

That attorney may have had a great idea. He may also have been right as to the best disposal of their equity. I seriously doubt, however, that he will ever be their most trusted advisor.

Coaching with Stories

Everyone loves stories. They are the oldest form of teaching and learning. Traveling story tellers were the communication vehicle for the spread of news, religion and entertainment for thousands of years. The ability to visualize a good story is genetically imprinted on most humans.

> The ability to visualize a good story is genetically imprinted on most humans.

Business owners are even bigger fans of stories than most folks. They like both success stories, as well as those where the message is more of, "There lie monsters," about other owners who made mistakes and the price they paid for them. That's because owners are every bit as concerned with avoiding disaster as they are with pursuing success.

More importantly, stories take the spotlight off of you, and ground your advice in real-world experience. It's very different to say, "I worked with a business similar to yours, and here is what they did." Rather than "I think you should do this," Whether the other client did it because of your advice or someone else's isn't relevant. They did it, it worked or it didn't, and that's a fact, rather than merely your opinion.

The longer you are in the advisory business, the more stories you'll have to tell. Being able to illustrate your questions and recommendations not only helps the client understand what you are describing, it helps to render a mental picture of a person and a situation they can empathize with.

THE COACHING DISCOVERY APPROACH

Set the ground rules. You have a mental picture of the coaching role, but it probably isn't the same as your client's. Describe specifically how your process works.

Always tell the truth. That means sometimes you have to challenge the client's statements or beliefs if you know them to be flawed.

Ask open-ended questions. Then ask <u>more</u> open-ended questions. Remember to WAIT. ("Why Am I Talking?")

Increase your ratio of listening to speaking. Two-to-one is a minimum. Practice trying for five-to-one, and ten-to-one is often desirable.

Use practical illustrations. Put numbers to the plan. Let the client change the numbers to better understand the impact.

Focus on communication styles. Deliberately modify your style to match the client's.

Don't be a showoff. Jargon and acronyms should follow the strategy, not precede it.

Tell stories. Real life-examples carry the most weight.

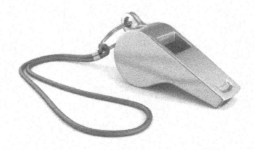

PART THREE: COACHING DISCOVERY
THE DELIVERABLES

Coaching is asking questions. Advising is providing answers. Within that framework we will discuss developing a client's exit strategy by asking questions. Note that I didn't say we will develop the exit plan.

An exit plan is a complex implementation schedule that involves time, multiple professionals and a coordinated approach. Whether the client is seeking value enhancement advice to increase the proceeds of a sale, training for successors, or just general legal and tax wisdom for an internal transaction, implementation requires a strategy.

This book is about helping a client choose that strategy and helping them understand what they can realistically expect as a result of it. The output of your work together is unique, since its creation is shared at every stage by the client, and the result is as much theirs as it is yours. The discovery process is experienced by both the advisor and the client.

The National Exit Planners Survey™ found that 96% of advisors expect continuing work to come from developing an exit strategy. The deliverable will identify areas where you can further assist in a comprehensive exit plan and is the jumping off point to the next phase of your advisory relationship.

This section is focused on the nuts and bolts of presenting a strategy that leads naturally to the next phase of your trusted advisor relationship.

1.4 The Owner's Initial Objective

"It's not the strongest of the species that survives, nor the most intelligent, but the one who responds most to change."

~ Charles Darwin

"I'll Just Sell It"

Most owners begin an exit planning process with an expectation about what they think should happen. Unfortunately, most of their opinions are wrong.

To start, 85% of business owners initially expect to sell their companies to a third party.[7] This is often the point where I have my first coaching conversation, and it happens before we even start an engagement. I'll ask, "What do you want from a planning process?"

The owner responds with something like, "I want to sell my company for five million dollars in three years."

Many advisors take those thirteen words as the start of a plan. The owner's objective is clear and concrete, but just agreeing to implement a client's initial plan falls short of your responsibility as an advisor. Coaching carries with it an obligation to make sure any client's idea has been properly vetted before moving forward with implementation. As a coach, it is your responsibility to ground their conversations in reality, even when that may be unpleasant for the client.

> As a coach, it's your responsibility to ground the clients' conversations in reality.

Starting a coaching relationship means not taking anything for granted. If you are going to be a truth-sayer, it helps a whole lot if you have some idea what the truth is. Here is what those thirteen words don't tell you.

- Why $5,000,000?
    - Is that pre or post tax?
    - Is the company worth that much? (Again, pre or post tax?)
    - Is that based on hearsay, your guess, or a professional analysis?
- What is the $5,000,000 for?
    - Is the plan to retire?
    - If so, is $5,000,000 enough?
    - Has the analysis been done on how long that will last considering longevity expectations, future medical needs, and inflation?
- Why did you choose a three-year timeframe?
    - Is that because you can't work longer than that? (Burnout, health, other commitments?)
    - Is that a hard walk-away date? (Meaning any transition periods must be greatly accelerated?)
    - What do you plan on doing with the business in that time frame?

That's <u>just</u> the questions that come from the owner's first *sentence*.

The Path of Least Resistance

When I was a business broker, we would frequently receive calls from former executives who had taken an early retirement, and wanted to purchase a business. When asked what type of business they would prefer, the most frequent answer by far was "light manufacturing."

Further questioning usually revealed that they had reached their conclusion by a process of elimination. As buyers, they weren't interested in the long hours and weekends required by most retail stores and restaurants. They didn't have a professional license, so architecture, engineering, law and accounting were out. These executives also didn't have a trade license, which eliminated electrical and plumbing contractors and numerous other licensed professions from welding to managed services for information networks.

They certainly ruled out heavy industry, or anything that involved pollution or government regulation. Trucking didn't sound like fun, nor did anything that required working outside in inclement weather such as landscaping, garbage collection or home repair.

So by process of elimination, light manufacturing was (to them,) a clear and obvious choice. The funny thing was, every one of them presented their objective as the result of great strategic analysis, regardless of their ignorance about manufacturing.

Business owners frequently go through a similar process of elimination. Perhaps they know that they aren't sufficiently differentiated to attract a strategic acquirer. They aren't large enough for private equity. A competitor might be interested, but they're terrified of prematurely letting the local market players know that they're considering a sale of the business.

I always ask whether the owner has employees that are capable of running the business on a day-to-day basis. If the answer is no, then we're probably going to have an issue finding a buyer who's willing to become the central decision point for daily operations. In some cases that may mean a lengthy employment or consulting contract to teach a new owner how to run the company. In the worst cases, owner centricity can make the business unsalable.

If they do have capable managers in place, the answer is typically, "They could run it, but they can't buy it because they have no money."

So by process of elimination, the owner has decided that his exit strategy will be a sale to a third party. Unless the business is light manufacturing <GRIN>, he has no idea of the odds he faces.

Explaining the Odds

I've extensively studied the numbers on third party sales, and they aren't very encouraging. Bear with me while I run through them to a logical conclusion. This is an exercise I do with many prospective clients.

1. Baby Boomers are reaching age 65 at a rate of about 10,000 a day. This number will be sustained through 2029.[8]

2. They also had (at their apex) the highest concentration ratio of business employers (5 or more employees) to their total population at about 6%.[9] That means about 600 business owners reach 65 daily.

3. Although some leave their businesses earlier or later than age 65, let's take the 600 per day as an average. That's over 220,000 exiting owners annually.

4. Since 2010, when I first started researching the Boomer transitions, the number of Boomer employers has dropped from about 4 million to roughly 3 million. That would imply that 182,000 owners are now exiting each year. Between the above projection and this one, let's use 182,000 as a more conservative handicapping of their odds for a third party sale.

5. According to the International Business Brokers' Association (IBBA), their members sell between 8,000 and 9,000 companies a year.[10] That number has been pretty consistent for the last decade.

6. The Private Equity (PE) market has grown rapidly, reaching an all-time high of about 3,500 transactions in 2021.[11] Since PE stats include a number of larger private companies of over $100 million in revenue, let's say that 3,000 of those deals are owner-managed businesses.

It's time to do the math. If 182,000 businesses a year are available for sale, and professional intermediaries account for 12,000 of those, there are 170,000 owners left to figure out their transition on their own. That is over 93% of all the theoretically available Boomer-owned companies every year.

> **93% of all Boomer-owned companies will need to develop an alternative exit plan.**

No one tracks the numbers on how those companies change hands, or even if they do. Certainly, some sales are facilitated by other professionals (mostly attorneys and accountants) who don't report to the intermediary industry. In some cases, owners walk away and leave the company in the hands of employees without being compensated at all.

A substantial number of the businesses close. The US Small Business Administration says that about 600,000 businesses close in a typical year. (800,000 during the COVID-19 pandemic.) Those numbers include about two-thirds of non-employer businesses (e.g. real estate partnerships and holding companies). That leaves about 200,000 employer businesses that close in an average year.

At present, 50% of employers of 5 or more people have owners between age 55 and 74.[12] Those tend to be businesses that are more stable and more successful. (Only about 25% of start-ups survive for 15 years or more.)[13] We can guess that most of the Boomer owners who are selling their businesses are in that 25% since they are most likely not start-ups. That would indicate roughly 50,000 closures annually.

> **At present, 50% of employers of 5 or more people have owners between age 55 and 74.**

In short, even the owners of strong, profitable companies who anticipate a sale to a third party still face substantial odds. After weeding out the closures, they have about an 80% chance (108,000 among the 120,000 remaining) of having to create their own path to a successful transfer.

Put it all together:

Business/Owner Categories	% Boomer Owned	Boomer Businesses
6,000,000 Employers (5+ employees)	50%	3,000,000
Annual number reaching 65 years old		182,000
Sold by Business Brokers		(9,000)
Acquired by Private Equity		(3,000)
Closed		(50,000)
Owners needing another exit plan		**120,000**

So 85% of owners are looking for a sale to a third party. Less than 7% will succeed with that strategy using traditional intermediaries. Your first obligation is to help your client understand why he or she needs to plan. Success in transferring any business is far from guaranteed.

> Success in transferring any business is far from guaranteed.

There are alternative exits to a third-party sale which we will discuss further on. From a coaching perspective, however, this is our first opportunity to help the client understand that disposing of the business isn't as straightforward as they might have anticipated.

If we haven't yet been engaged, we are showing the prospect two things. First, that we have knowledge he or she didn't know and never considered. Second, as coaches we are not afraid to stick pins in inflated assumptions.

Setting Client Expectations

When we coach advisors on how to land new engagements by using our ExitMap® Assessment©, we focus particularly on the anomalies between the owner's different responses and any mistaken assumptions. That is where we begin to set the expectations for our relationship. Even though we will usually save the discussion of mistaken beliefs regarding value until later on, other presumptions must be addressed at the outset.

One of those is the idea that any good business can find a buyer if they just look hard enough for one. Any business broker will tell you that there is a buyer out there for every business but in reality, brokers fail to find a buyer for about 80% of their listings.[14]

Developing an exit plan that meets the expectations of an owner will never happen if those expectations can't possibly be met. The first step in developing a plan that makes owners happy a year (and even longer) after their exit is to reach an understanding about what you can do for them, and what they can reasonably expect as a result. That requires grounding them in reality.

Owners should be cautious of any advisor who agrees with their exit goals without supporting evidence. That may sound obvious, but it frequently doesn't happen.

Everyone likes to be agreed with. Some advisors believe that the secret to getting an engagement is to agree with everything the prospective client says.

> **Some advisors believe that the secret to getting an engagement is to agree with everything the prospective client says.**

"You want to retire in two years? We can help you with that." The advisor knows (or should) that a relatively short time frame like two years requires considerable sophistication in the management team, strong financial history, and solid documentation of processes.

"You want to leave with $10,000,000? That sounds reasonable." How would the advisor know? Regardless of the apparent size and success of a business, perhaps profitability is poor, or the financial statements are a mess. The owner may want to sell because of new competition, or because there are issues with a customer who represents a majority of the revenue.

Unfortunately, many will agree to the client's goals and worry if they are realistic later. That's not the road to becoming a trusted advisor.

In Robert A. Heinlein's classic 1961 science fiction novel *Stranger in a Strange Land* the attorney Jubal Harshaw employs Anne, a Fair Witness who is licensed to testify before the High Court. She is trained to observe, and only report what she knows to be an irrefutable fact. Harshaw demonstrates her training with a simple question.

> Jubal: "That new house on the far hilltop – can you see what color they've painted it?"
>
> Anne: "It's white on this side."
>
> Jubal: "You see? Anne is so thoroughly indoctrinated that it doesn't even occur to her to infer that the other side is probably white too. (No one) …could force her to commit to the far side unless she herself went around to the other side and looked."

A good coach tries as much as possible to emulate a Fair Witness, while business owners can take hearsay for gospel. They can over or underestimate their understanding of circumstances. They may generalize and make assumptions using sparse data. It's the coach's responsibility to determine what is true and what is conjecture. An exit plan built on speculation is a recipe for disaster.

15 The Personal Vision

> *"Most people get excited about games, but I've got to be excited about practice, because that's my classroom."*
> ~ Pat Summit

Visioning the Future

The owner's personal vision is the most important, and frequently the most neglected component of a successful exit plan. The 75% or so of unhappy owners aren't unhappy because their companies sold for less than they were worth. For many, if not most, it is because they didn't know what to expect from life after the business.

Coaching an owner until he or she has developed a viable personal vision for life without the business can be a challenge, but it is the core deliverable of any exit planning.

> **Entrepreneurs have to be excited about the future.**

Entrepreneurs have to be excited about the future. It's what drives them to succeed.

How do you expect any business owner to be excited about a future where he doesn't understand his identity, or what will keep her busy, or how they will generate the fulfillment and satisfaction they currently enjoy from solving problems, developing people, and winning deals?

Every certification program and book about exiting discusses the importance of having a plan for life following the exit. Yet, many advisors skip over this issue as if it will solve itself after the more "important" work of transferring the company is completed. They dutifully ask the client, "What will you do after you sell the business?" The client responds, "I am going to play a lot of golf!" They both laugh, and the advisor mentally checks off the "life after the business" box on the exit planning checklist.

That isn't good enough. Very few people can fill their days with nothing but golf. Even fewer would argue that improving their handicap qualifies as a life purpose. An owner's Personal Vision, and I cannot stress this enough, needs to be more detailed, more practical, and more attractive than that.

Filling in Their Week

Here is a coaching exercise we do with our exit planning clients.

Calculate the amount of time that the client currently spends at the business. (It is one of the key questions on the ExitMap® Assessment©, and one we teach our subscribers to focus on.) Include that "quiet time" at the beginning or end of the day when they like to think, but don't consider it "working." Add in answering emails and texts at home or reading reports and articles on the weekend. Conservatively speaking, most owners are engaged with their business, whether physically or just mentally, for at least 50 hours a week, or roughly 2,500 hours a year.

Now, let's try to fill that same amount of time with things that they plan to do in retirement. Start with golf every Monday, Wednesday, and Friday. It takes about 5 hours to play a leisurely 18-hole round. That's a lot of golf, but we have only consumed about 15 hours of the work week. What else?

Many folks will say they want to do more community service. Unless they plan to take on the full-time responsibility of running a charitable organization, let's try some simple volunteering to start. Two half-days every week? That's considerable dedication to a cause, but even then only consumes another eight hours. We are up to twenty-three hours, or about half their current work week.

Travel is a big goal for many owners. We suggest a full, two-week vacation every quarter. Even if the owner doesn't demur ("Oh, that's too much!"), each vacation would absorb about 100 hours of their current annual work schedule. If total vacations covered 400 working hours a year, that's an average of another 8 hours a week. We are up to thirty-one hours of "things to do."

Exercise and get into better shape is another objective high on the list of retirement activities for many self-neglecting entrepreneurs. Let's throw in five mornings a week at the gym. That's thirty-six.

Now you have two months of traveling (400 hours,) 150 golf outings (750 hours,) 5 hours a week at the gym (250 hours annually) and 50 days a year (400 hours) spent on community service or charities. The total is 2,000 hours, even if we double-dip by assuming vacation occurs in addition to the other routine activities.

That still leaves you with about 700 hours, or 14 hours a week to fill. What is left? Sleep in and catch up on your reading at a book a week? Have lunch with the spouse every day?

There are lots of ways to fill the remaining time, but remember our example started with someone who already had a lot of plans. Many business owners have none. And, we are also assuming that none of these activities will ever get old.

ExitMap® Express™ tools include an interactive form that allows subscribers to conduct this exercise together with the client. It asks questions about planned activities and major purchases, then assigned weekly time requirements for the activities initial costs and maintenance for the purchases.

The Personal Vision Builder™ automatically applies the times and costs to the client's post-ownership plan to illustrate the impact of each decision.

> When they say, "I want a lot of money," we ask, "How much is a lot?"

This simple exercise is an example of the coaching relationship. We start with where the client is now, ask where he wants to go, and have him describe what it looks like when he gets there. It's the coach's job to qualify nebulous ideas, to make them more tangible. When they say, "I want a lot of money," we ask, "How much is a lot?" When they say, "As soon as possible," we say, "Give me a deadline."

The coach's job is to help the client move from vague "wants" to concrete goals. Once an owner sees the objectives in writing he often changes them. You can avoid a lot of extra work by creating an outline of what the strategy entails.

We think this outline is so important, we've built it into the ExitMap® Express™ process. There is an entire meeting dedicated to just going over the major strategy points in outline form. Occasionally an advisor will opine that it is a waste of a meeting. When that was brought up in a training call, one of our subscribers said, "I've done 25 planning engagements with ExitMap. I have never, ever, presented an outline to a client and *not* had him make changes."

Going over an outline, or as we call it internally a "This is what I heard you say" meeting, is critical. It's the first time the client sees all the components in one place. Changes are easily made. You avoid spending additional time on details that may be thrown out later.

Most importantly you get the client's input before they see the final plan. I would much rather present an outline two or three times than hit the "Wait a minute" moment when I'm reviewing the final report and their complete strategy.

Components of the Vision
The owner's personal vision has two aspects, tangible benefits and intangible benefits.

Tangible benefits are what you might expect. They could include a second home, boat, airplane or exotic trip. We list these with an approximate cost. This should be included in the client's expectations for retirement funding.

> The owner's personal vision has two aspects, tangible benefits and intangible benefits.

Intangible benefits are more difficult to nail down. They usually involve time like rounds of golf or weeks of vacation. The attraction of those activities tends to wear off over time. It's far better, and more effective, to focus on activities that bring with them a sense of purpose.

Here are a few suggestions to help coaches and owners begin thinking about purpose.

Make the world a better place. This could be as simple as volunteering at the local food bank, or as complex as going on a mission to a third-world country.

Self-improvement. Learn to play a musical instrument, read the great novels, study a martial art or oriental meditation, undertake a fitness regimen or become a docent for a museum or national monument. Go back to school.

Teach and mentor. Become an adjunct professor in the local community college. Volunteer for S.C.O.R.E. or the local SBDC, join Big Brothers/Big Sisters, or start a peer group for smaller business owners.

It's important to fill in the details. Few people want to rush out and volunteer on the day after they leave their business, but neglecting to set the goal is the first step to not doing anything. Set a time frame to start. Create an investigative process to determine what fits and what doesn't.

Practice, Practice, Practice

Remember, part of any coach's job is to get the players to practice.

The ExitMap® Assessment© questionnaire is completed by every one of our potential exit planning clients. The first two questions are critical because they help to determine the client's exit time frames. They are, "When do you want to step back from day-to-day responsibilities?" and "When do you want to leave the business entirely?"

The truth is, once we've helped an owner accomplish the first objective, stepping back, the time frame for the second frequently gets pushed out.

> Once we've helped an owner accomplish the first objective, the second frequently gets pushed out.

107

When entering into a long-term planning relationship, I initially try to help the owner rearrange their responsibilities so that they can take off one day a week. I then encourage the owner to use that day to practice for life after the business. It can be spent cycling, woodworking, or working in a local charity.

The important point is to have them do it on a regular basis and see how long it retains their interest.

Two "Good" Obstacles to Exit Planning Implementation

When advising business owners, it's vital to take into consideration their attachment to the business. This is such a critical issue that it is worth mentioning again.

An advisor spends a lot of time and energy with the client developing the vision for life after ownership in the hopes that it is far more attractive to them than their current role in the business.

Yet no matter how well developed that vision is, or how well defined the action steps are, it isn't unusual to find owners who behave in a way that ultimately sabotages their plans. Sometimes their actions are even intentional, but more often they aren't. The problems arise in two ways.

"Death by Inattention"

As I said previously, we have two target dates. The first is when they want to be relieved of day-to-day operational responsibilities. The second is when they want to be completely free of any connection to the company.

We tell clients that once we have achieved the first objective, the second may become more flexible. Freed of the task-based duties of running the business, owners often become more strategic. They may start planning for new growth and value creation. They might go back to their role when the business first started, when they were the best salesperson or designer of novel product offerings.

Owners returning to their core skill set usually benefits the business. The problem arises when they enjoy the lack of responsibility so much that they become owners in absentia.

There is no strategy. The company drifts along on the backs of the operations managers, but really doesn't have any direction beyond "more of what we did yesterday." There are no new initiatives.

Companies are organic. They are either growing or shrinking. The lack of direction may take a while to have an impact, but eventually performance will suffer. Getting owners to reengage after time away from the responsibilities of running the business can be exceedingly difficult, but if they don't jump back in, the transition is unlikely to accomplish their longer-term objectives.

"Death by Over-Attention"

The second obstacle to successfully implementing a transition occurs after owners have surrendered their task-based duties. In this case, they are unable to define their contribution in the absence of being "busy." They begin looking for ways to contribute, sometimes where their contribution isn't needed.

It's not uncommon to begin demanding more accountability and greater detail than is really necessary. They pour over reports looking for errors, anomalies or declining results in an attempt to prove their value.

Another common technique that might be used to prove contribution is "seagull management." An owner may look for opportunities to make decisions, but does it without consulting the managers who are in charge of the function. Because they have always known best, they still know best. What isn't as obvious is that they are now working in a vacuum, with little knowledge of what went before. The results are not ideal.

A third way owners might evidence over-attention is with a "break the rules" mentality. They offer exemptions from policy, or circumnavigate systems because they *can*. Exercising authority shows who is in charge, even if they show little concern for any resulting disruption in the business.

Preventing the Two Obstacles

We call them "good" obstacles because they typically occur only after some level of initial success in the exit planning process. That is, the owner has at least partially stepped away from the day-to-day responsibilities of the business. But the obstacles are a direct result of relieving the owner of those more mundane management duties. Each is preventable with some preparation.

> Inattention and over-attention can be forestalled by including a tangible description of the owner's next level of responsibility in the planning process.

Inattention and over-attention can be forestalled by including a tangible description of the owner's next level of responsibility in the planning process. If the owner resists retained responsibilities, then the future becomes plain. Plans can then include transfer of higher functions to the management team. If the owner insists on retaining a level of day-to-day control, the coaching process should include defined parameters about what reporting is really necessary, and how often it will be presented.

In either case, the problems occur when the owner is crossing the no man's land between total focus on the business and the time when it isn't a recipient of their attention at all. Like any no man's land, it is unfamiliar territory, and some pathfinding is necessary. That is the coach's job.

16 Delegation and Depth

"Fail early, fail often, but always fail forward."
~ John Maxwell

Owner Centricity

Owner centricity is the single biggest value killer in any business. No one wants to acquire a company that requires them to work 70 hours a week to take home a paycheck. The client's claimed work week hours are one of the first factors I look at when debriefing an ExitMap® Assessment©. If they spend over 55 hours working, we tell the prospect up front that managing their personal work habits is going to be the biggest challenge of our engagement.

An owner who works a lot more than a "normal" 40 hour week doesn't have a company; they have a job. Given the unlikely probability that he can find a buyer, the purchase is almost inevitably going to come with the requirement that he work as an employee for an extended period to provide training and a cohesive transition.

I have also heard owners who are planning an internal succession claim, "it would take at least two employees to replace me." In such cases the delta between the owners income and benefits, less the salary of an extra employee to share their job, should be deducted from any future cash flow estimation. That may be a sobering exercise for the owner.

> "It would take at least two employees to replace me."

The Small Business Start-Up

When the founder of a company starts out, there is little choice about learning the different skills required to keep a business functioning. The owner is usually the first salesperson. She is the one approaching customers and selling her vision as to why they should do business with her.

Once a prospect becomes a customer, this new owner is most often the one who has to deliver the goods or services purchased. She is in charge of warranty, customization, and follow up. She also has to do the billing and collect payment on the sale.

On a positive note, running a start-up is relatively flexible and forgiving. If you get a few weeks behind in your invoicing, an evening of burning the midnight oil can get you caught up. If you deliver the wrong item, it's usually a quick trip to make an exchange. If you have a week without any sales, you might just skip your paycheck to make ends meet.

It is perfectly understandable how the owner of a Main Street business becomes a multi-position player. Unfortunately, it is all too frequently the reason why they are still running a Main Street business. The challenge of being your own indispensable employee is that you are the biggest obstacle to growth.

Planning for succession is doomed to fail if the owner is looking for a "mini me" to fill their shoes. A friend terms that type of search as "seeking the flying mermaid." You want someone who can manage employees, maintain a bigger portfolio of business than anyone else in the company, and balance the books in their spare time. Such people can be made by dint of necessity or by trial and error, but they are unlikely to be available as a buyer. (Most of them are already running a small business of their own!)

If the business has gone beyond the Main Street level without addressing owner centricity, it simply exacerbates the problem. Each individual function of sales, management, or accounting has become too important to be done in someone's spare time. The cost of an error when the average sale is $100 is far different than when the average sale is $10,000. Mismanaging 3 employees is more recoverable than mismanaging 30.

So the first thing an owner needs to accept is the fact that a well-trained management team brings far more value in an acquisition than a superstar owner.

It's the Management, Stupid!

In initial or Phase One engagements we always include an assessment of the management team. While many advisors will analyze revenue growth, margins compared to industry norms, or marketing and customer mix, these all pale in comparison to the importance of having capable management personnel.

> Operational improvements pale in comparison to the importance of having capable management personnel.

Without strong management of the sales function the greatest product in the world will not find its way into the hands of customers. Without appropriate oversight of production the company's costs will exceed that of their competitors, and their profitability will be worse. Without savvy oversight of the cash flow, the business is begging to careen from crisis to crisis.

We have the owner complete the Owner Centricity™ online assessment (available for free at ownercentricity.com). It contains questions about their personal responsibility and level of participation in 75 functional areas of the company. It is simple and quick. The owner only needs to place a check in one of four columns, based on their own role in that function.

1. Principal: In this area of the business, you initiate actions and make decisions largely by yourself.

2. Approval: Decisions are usually made by others, but must be approved by you before implementation.

3. Delegated: Decisions are made and implemented by others, results are reported to you.

4. N/A: You don't have this function in your business.

Once completed, the automatically-generated report helps identify major areas where the company depends on the owner's direct involvement in operational duties and functions. The ultimate goal being to delegate those responsibilities so that the owner can step away.

To build on this exercise we transfer the results to a Management Succession spreadsheet that lists the same 75 tasks. It has fields that identify a primary and secondary responsible party for each area. The owner's name is filled in the primary field wherever it was checked as "Principal." Key employees assigned that responsibility are filled in everywhere else.

As we work through this exercise with the owner entering the names of the person primarily responsible, we also identify the person who is backing them up. The selections are made from a pull down menu of the key employees' names. The backup is then ranked as one, two, or three.

One means that the backup person is fully capable of assuming this position. A 2 means that the backup person would be qualified to assume the responsibility if they were properly trained. A 3 means that there is no backup, or the backup person has no idea how to handle the responsibility of that position.

As we enter 1, 2, or 3, in the Management Succession spreadsheet, it automatically fills in green for one, yellow for two, or red for those tasks ranked three. The outcome is a listing showing quite clearly where the weakest areas of the management team are, and what responsibilities need the most attention.

These simple tools give an owner an overview of where the team is weak, what the training priorities need to be, and where there may be a need for recruiting new talent into the company. This highly visual red-yellow-green methodology tells both the owner and the advisor how far away the company's management is from being fully prepared for a transition.

Reverse Depression

In my second book, *Hunting in a Farmer's World*, I coined the term "reverse depression" to describe the way an owner often feels when it appears he or she is no longer needed.

It's a poor descriptor, but in the seven years since *Hunting's* publication I have failed to come up with a better term. It goes something like this:

> *"I just came back from a two week vacation. My phone rang with a call from the business exactly twice, and both calls were just to check with me before a manager finalized a decision. Both the decisions were fine. On my return there were no notes requesting my attention from employees, and no panicky voice mails requiring my intervention. I made the rounds of all my managers to see if they needed help from me. None did.*
>
> *I've spent the last 26 years working my tail off to develop a management team that could put me in this kind of position as an owner. Somehow, I thought it would feel a lot better than this."*

While most owners will hopefully wrestle with this feeling at some point, they usually recognize that it's something to overcome. Others, however, suffer from decision addiction.

Owner Centricity and Decision Addiction

Every business owner must be adept at dealing with chaos.

Entrepreneurship demands the ability to choose a course of action when everyone else is staring into the headlights. It requires a willingness to make a decision with inadequate information, and to make new decisions if the first one isn't solving the problem.

Being a business owner means rolling with the punches. How often do owners enter their business in the morning with a detailed idea of their day's objectives, only to have them go out the window as soon as they arrive? A key employee calls in sick. A customer is in crisis. A vendor is unable to deliver as promised. A piece of equipment is broken. There are scores of processes that go right day after day, but if one of them fails, the ability of the owner to plan often fails with it.

In small businesses, problems flow upwards. Harry Truman famously had a sign on his desk that said, "The Buck Stops Here." Business owners know that is part of the job. A good employee comes in and tells you that something has gone wrong. It was his responsibility, and he admits that the fault was his. It doesn't matter. It may be his fault, but it is your consequence. The owner can't ignore it, and he can't wait for someone else to work it out. As the owner, it immediately becomes his job to resolve it, or to direct someone who can.

> Owners build processes to stop problems before they happen.

Owners build processes to stop problems before they happen. They produce checklists, redundancies, quality measures and reports. When those fail, however, it is their job to fix it and prevent it from happening again. That is their core skill, the one thing that employees seldom want to assume, even though it's the one thing most owners would most like to delegate.

For many owners, that core skill becomes the one thing they have confidence in. They become addicted to the adrenalin of firefighting. They complain about their employees' inability to see problems before they occur. They rail against the need to jump in and be the fixer, but the truth is, they love it. The role of chief problem solver is the main component of their irreplaceable skill set. It is the one thing in the company that no one else can do. It's their job security.

As with any addiction, the "user" claims he can stop any time he wishes. Owners pine for the day when they can just run the company. "I'd like to get to the point where I just think about strategic issues," they say. "I want to spend more time on planning, more time on new markets, more time on developing people, but I'm stuck fixing day-to-day problems instead."

Is that true, or are they addicted to being the place where the buck stops? There is a little rush that comes with beating a crisis. There is a sense of self-worth when you say, "I was the only one who could have taken care of that." If you do it often enough, you risk becoming a dopamine junkie.

We discussed this briefly in chapter one, from the perspective of the decision-making rush. This is where in the planning process we examine the result – a weak management team.

For any business to grow, someone other than the owner has to be able to solve problems. Is the owner filling that role because they have to, or simply because they can? Firefighting is a necessary skill, but if it's the main thing that an owner brings to the table, they are the biggest enemy of their own success. It's difficult to look in the mirror and admit that you are the problem.

It's the coach's job to be that mirror and to say, "You may not be the fairest of them all."

17 Beyond Coaching

"Winning isn't a some-time thing. It's an all-time thing."
~ Vince Lombardi

The Next Phase

If you've developed your trusted advisor relationship by coaching, the next phase of discovery involves presenting your jointly developed strategy along with the practical recommendations for moving forward with its implementation.

With most planning or value enhancement software, this is done through a series of recommendations. These recommendations represent actual tasks where courses of action must be undertaken in order to make the plan reality.

At ExitMap® we guide advisors through the recommendation process by asking a series of questions around the four functional areas from the original Exit Readiness Assessment. The potential recommendations are not comprehensive. They are broad and designed to easily be supplemented with additional ideas from the advisor's own area of expertise.

Possible Financial Recommendations

- Does the client need a professionally prepared valuation for the business?
- Can or should the company develop financial KPIs, a budget, cash flow analysis or improved financial reporting?
- Should the company be seeking new credit facilities?
- Should there be a schedule for reducing or eliminating personal guarantees?

- Would common size or other financial analyses identify expenses that are growing disproportionately to revenues?
- Does the company have a funded buy/sell agreement?
- Does the company have insurance for business interruption, key employees, owner disability or wage continuation?
- Is restructuring required for tax planning or asset protection?

Possible Planning Recommendations
- Does the client need to "practice" their involvement in activities, organizations or hobbies in preparation for life after the business?
- Does the company need business continuity instructions?
- Should the client develop a work schedule that includes non-business activities away from the office, with a gradually increasing time allotment and a target date for elimination of day-to-day management activities?
- Should the client develop transfer schedules for management duties, ownership responsibilities, outside relationships, chain of command and employee or family skills development?
- Does the client need a will, estate plan, or comprehensive financial planning?

Possible Revenue and Profit Recommendations
- Should the company develop a sales strategy for new products or markets?
- Does the sales strategy require new vendors, personnel, or capabilities?
- Would the company benefit from an analysis of competitors, product line profitability or profit by customer class?
- Is there an opportunity to develop recurring revenue through service contracts, "Just in Time" supply agreements, or warranties?

- Can customer or vendor relationships be better secured with formal contracts?
- Is the company sales incentive system current and motivating to those working under it?
- Is there a need to engage better bidding or estimating skills?
- Is there a need to train in better selling or sales management skills?
- Is there an opportunity to create differentiation from competitors?
- Should the company upgrade or revamp its purchasing systems?

Possible Operations Recommendations

- Are there recommended training programs for the management team?
- Does the company need an audit or update of its employment manual, operating procedures or incentive programs?
- Should any employees have stay bonuses, profit based incentives, retention agreements, virtual equity or nonqualified deferred compensation plans?
- Does the company need assistance in developing core values, a mission statement or a vision?
- Does the company require consulting assistance in upgrading its technology?
- Should the company conduct a salary study of market and industry compensation rates?
- Does the company need a plan for developing new management capabilities, or to develop a plan that replaces the owner's centricity?

Closing the Implementation Engagement

It's obvious from the laundry list of recommendations above that most transition plans have a level of complexity that allows ample opportunity for any consultant to find appropriate work. It should be equally obvious that there is no single consultant capable of effectively delivering everything on the list.

The presentation of your coaching discovery deliverable, coupled with your recommendations, should make closing an engagement for the next phase of work a matter of course. In keeping with the coaching philosophy of asking more questions before delivering any advice, I recommend asking the following after reviewing the list of recommendations with the client.

1. Which of these areas do you feel we should address first?
2. Which recommendations most concern you regarding difficulty of implementation?
3. Where do you think I can be of the greatest assistance to you?
4. Is there anything else you need from me before we get started with the next phase?
5. Would you like me to prepare a proposal for the next phase of our work together?

18. It Takes a Team

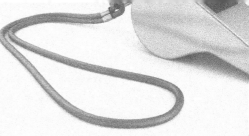

"An acre of performance is worth a whole world of promise."
~ Red Auerbach

Coaching is One-on-One

Coaching is by its nature a one-on-one activity. Although we subscribe to the industry-wide acceptance of a team approach to comprehensive exit planning, we frequently do not "read in" other advisors until we are sure that we've identified the client's main objectives.

Typically, we ask if there are other advisors that the client wants to involve in his planning. We will then reach out to them to let them know that we are working on a transition strategy with the client. We will also ask them about specific technical questions in their areas of expertise, usually those involving taxation or legal issues.

We don't, however, bring them into our initial coaching discovery process until we have spent ample time helping the client define the objectives. Although few advisors are as aggressively single-minded as the GRAT enthusiast attorney in chapter 13, most have opinions about which components in their area of expertise would be best utilized in a transition strategy.

An initial strategy is usually improved with the input of other professionals but not at the outset. When you start out with a number of cooks, each contributing their own favorite ingredient, the meal is unlikely to be a combination of complimentary dishes. Our objective in coaching discovery is to insulate the clients from the temptation to try and accommodate <u>all</u> of the advice they receive.

> **An initial strategy is usually improved with the input of other professionals.**

We know enough about the technical issues in a transition to point out obvious anomalies or flaws. A client may wish to negotiate long term guaranteed employment contracts with a buyer for favored employees. These would obviously pose legal issues, but we don't need to bring in an attorney to simply explain why an idea isn't feasible.

Similarly, we've encountered CPAs who have little background in the practical issues of negotiating a sale. But they tell their clients, "Only agree to a sale of stock so that you can realize a capital gains tax rate. Under no circumstances should you accept an offer of an asset sale." While that may be the basis of a sound tax reduction strategy, the client needs to understand that his CPA has absolutely no control over what a buyer is willing to offer.

Once we are confident that our coaching discovery has helped the client create a strategy that represents their needs and issues, then and only then, is it time to bring in the rest of this team.

Building the Team
Every exit requires a variety of specialty skills. Since sports analogies are endemic to business, many owners refer to their business strategy as a game plan. There are winners and losers. They "score" goals in sales or production.

As an advisor, you already know much of this. This chapter is simply to review the make-up of the team as it fits into a coaching approach.

Except for the smallest entrepreneurial businesses, most companies have a management team. They have assignments and areas of responsibility. Each team member is expected to contribute in their own areas, and support the efforts of the other team members with different responsibilities.

An exit advisory team functions the same way. If they are working together for a common goal, supporting each other, and taking direction from a single leader, success is far more likely. If they are each working in a vacuum, making decisions on the client's behalf without paying any attention to the actions other advisors are recommending, the client will spend a lot more money and inevitably have an inferior result.

Nothing impacts the success of a business transition more than the advisor team. Let's say you receive an invitation to lead a team to play in the Super Bowl. You know you will be playing against the Green Bay Packers, and you can choose any player not on their roster for your team. Who would you pick?

There are a multitude of opinions about who is the best quarterback, wide receiver or free safety in the NFL. One thing is pretty certain. You wouldn't choose the guys you grew up playing touch football with. At least, not if you wanted to win.

Let's take a look at who has to be on the team, who might be needed, and who should be on the field only at the appropriate time. Until we understand the functions of the team, we can't discuss the role of the coach.

Qualifying your Teammates

Owners often feel loyalty to the advisors they already have relationships with. "He's the attorney who handles all my legal problems," is a bit like saying, "He's the doctor I always go to when I feel sick." That is fine, but what if you needed a heart transplant?

All physicians went to medical school. In residency, they took rotations in surgery, obstetrics, pediatrics and infectious diseases. That doesn't mean that twenty years down the road you want someone delivering your newborn baby unless he's practiced it *a lot*.

Just as there are many physicians, there are also many attorneys and CPAs. They all have some training in all aspects of law or accounting.

It is required to pass the bar or to get certified. But if the attorney spent the last twenty years doing real estate closings, or the CPA spends most of his time preparing tax returns, he or she may not be the right advisor for the biggest financial transaction of an owner's life.

Advisors who are more confident in the strength of their relationship with the client, or more successful in their specialty, will say "I don't do enough of this type of work to be fully confident of doing the best job for you. Let me recommend someone who has more expertise."

There are few things that make me happier in an engagement than an advisor who says, "This is really outside my area of expertise. I recommend you find someone else." I will tell any other professional that I recommend under those conditions that he must agree to "hands off" soliciting of the client's business outside his specialty area. Most are happy to agree to such professional courtesy.

Business transitions aren't simple. Even the asset sale of a small business has tax pitfalls that can easily trap those who don't know what to look for. I recently heard a story about an owner who sold the stock of his company to a large public entity. He was ecstatic about getting the lower capital gains tax rate and put that money aside for when he filed his IRS return.

> Over a year after the closing the seller saw his capital gains turned largely into ordinary income.

Unfortunately, neither his real estate attorney nor his tax-preparer CPA thought to include a prohibition against the buyer declaring a Section 338 (h) 10 election. While not common, it allows a buyer to recast the transaction as an asset purchase. The seller has little say in the matter unless such election has been identified (and prohibited) in the contracts. Over a year after the closing the seller saw his capital gains turned largely into ordinary income. It meant the money he put aside for taxes was about 20% short of the actual amount due.

The Impact of Bad Advice

A traditional CPA can continue to do the client's tax returns. A traditional attorney can still take care of the normal business and personal legal needs. For a transaction, however, it is imperative to bring in someone who deals with the sale and transfer of companies on a very regular basis.

Any competent CPA can tell you the difference between ordinary income tax and capital gains. Far fewer can suggest ways to structure transactions to move income from one tax category to another.

An inexperienced professional may create huge issues. I was coaching a client who was acquiring a lumber yard in a small town, well out in a rural area of Texas. The CPA for the sellers was a local tax preparer. Their business was one of the tax preparers biggest clients. I was reviewing the deal for my client, but wasn't directly involved in the transaction.

The owners had spent years writing down their inventory asset for "shrinkage and damage" well beyond what was actually missing or spoiled. Conveniently, the deductions amounted to the bulk of their tax liability each year. By the time of the sale transaction, there was roughly $800,000 in "missing" inventory in the yard.

The sellers' CPA came up with an idea to defer taxes. He recommended selling the inventory as a separate transaction, to be paid via a ten-year installment note. He explained to his client that their capital gains tax would only be due when paid, and they could realize additional interest income on the note.

> The sale of the "found" inventory would trigger depreciation recovery.

When I reviewed the structure, my alarm bells went off. I explained to my client that the sale of the "found" inventory would trigger depreciation recovery. In the IRS' view, that means you took deductions from taxable income in the past, and owe ordinary income tax on the recovery.

More importantly, depreciation recovery cannot be paid with an installment note. Where the CPA was telling his client that their first year tax obligation would be about $16,000 (capital gains on the first payment of $80,000,) their actual liability would be in the $320,000 range (40% of $800,000.) Unfortunately, they would have only received $80,000 for the first installment on the inventory note.

I was pretty sure that if the transaction was scrutinized by Internal Revenue (not uncommon in a business sale,) lawsuits would be flying in short order.

I told my client to ask their accountant to check his approach. He replied tersely that he was a licensed CPA, and knowing about taxes was his profession. I asked again, with the same response. Finally I wrote out the problem to be presented to the accountant.

He returned a few days later and mumbled something about a "recent change in the code that I must have missed." (The code on that issue has been the same for at least a few decades.)

Unfortunately, the sellers were so shocked at the impact of their many years of deferred taxes, they backed out of the deal.

Similarly, most business attorneys can write (or download) a purchase agreement. Picking a reasonable path through the demands of the buyer's attorney for every representation, warranty and indemnification imaginable is another matter entirely, especially if the other attorney has more experience in transaction law.

The other issue is often cost. I'm regularly dismayed when I ask why someone uses a particular professional, and they answer, "Because he's inexpensive." Would they pick a heart surgeon using that criteria? Good help costs money.

Selling a company is a business owner's financial Super Bowl. He or she wants to put together the best advisor team possible for that *one game*. Afterwards, they can still go have a beer with their buddies from the sandlot. They will still be friends, and a good advisor will (or should) understand.

As the coach, you have an obligation to help the owner put the best team possible in the field. Discuss this with the client at the outset, and get their agreement to at least listen to your opinions.

The Starters

There are several tiers of necessity when it comes to team members. On the first tier are those without whom you cannot execute a transaction.

> **Transaction attorney** - One who knows the ins and outs of transferring a business. This should include converting customer and vendor contracts, required notifications of regulatory authorities, state law regarding notices to employees, as well as the aforementioned contract experience.
>
> **A forward-looking accountant** - Some business people would say that is an oxymoron. Most accountants, after all, make a living by telling clients what has already happened. Unfortunately, once a transaction is completed it is usually too late to do much tax planning. I look for someone who can make suggestions, and does so in the very first conversation.
>
> **A coach** - Whether the planned transfer is to family, employees, or a third party buyer, the owner's most important job is to keep running a healthy business. The coach keeps things on track. They keep in contact with the other professionals and they enforce deadlines. Ideally, besides being the project manager, the coach knows enough about the technical components of transfers to lend experience and ideas.

The coach might be an exit planner, a business coach, a consultant, the attorney, the accountant, or any other qualified professional whom the owner trusts. They must acknowledge the responsibility for coordinating the deal and driving it forward. That includes holding the owner accountable when necessary!

The Special Teams

At the most basic level the triumvirate of an attorney, an accountant, and somebody who is singularly focused on protecting the owner's interests is sufficient to complete many transactions. There are other players with specific skills who may not be directly involved in the transfer of the business, but whose skills are often needed.

> **Estate planning attorney -** Someone who is knowledgeable about wills, trusts, and multigenerational protection of assets can sometimes impact the deal structure with their perspective. More often, the estate planning attorney is working downstream of the transaction, protecting the proceeds of the most important financial event in the client's life.
>
> **Appraiser -** A valuation specialist may be necessary to place a defensible value on the company when the price may not be acceptable to other stakeholders or the IRS.
>
> **Business intermediary -** Many people would say that a business broker or investment banker should be one of the starters. This is an area where I strongly disagree about including them on the initial strategy team. People who sell businesses to third parties have a vested financial interest in only one type of exit strategy. While their advice can be invaluable in lending a buyer's point of view to the preparation of the company for sale, it is only the case when a third party sale has been previously decided as the owner's best strategy.
>
> **Financial planner -** Like the estate planning attorney, the financial planner may have excellent input on methods of receiving and distributing the proceeds of the sale. They are less likely to have useful advice about how a sale is

constructed, although in some cases could offer additional insight into the client's motives. If the financial planner has a long-term relationship with the client, a conversation is advisable early in the process.

Business growth consultant - If achieving the client's objectives requires that the business increases in value, it may call for the addition of someone who specializes in value enhancement. There are a number of excellent programs for building management accountability, capital or financing strategies, and employee motivation. In recent years several of the most popular of these systems have moved into certifying consultants as competent to deliver their particular programs.

"Value enhancement" is a simple term, but as a coach, your obligation is to help the owner select an approach that aligns with his or her strategy. A company that needs help in documenting processes may not require a sales trainer.

Risk management - Once a strategy is determined, there may be a need to assess the risks of non-completion due to the death or illness of a key participant. While there are some very specific risk management experts, most are licensed insurance brokers. They can help mitigate the issues involved if their party (buyer or seller) in the transaction is unable to complete the plan. These professionals are especially important when considering internal transfers, where the buyer and seller have little financial resources outside the company.

On the Sidelines

Most professional sports teams have specialty coaches to assist with certain technical aspects of the game. They may be deeply analytical of a player's throwing motion, jump shot, or swing. They focus on that area and that area only.

Similarly, there are business experts who may be called in only when a specific issue or goal warrants it.

Family business psychologists - These are specialists who deal with the dynamics of a family owned business. Conflicts among multiple owners in a company can be exacerbated by family relationships. These specialists approach the business from the family perspective, and deal with the underlying issues in personal relationships that are impacting the company.

Compensation specialists - These consultants may focus on supplemental retirement, nonqualified deferred compensation, or sales commission structures. They are often experts in the use of insurance and other funding methodologies for equity appreciation-based retention programs and profit sharing mechanisms.

ESOP specialists - Employee Stock Ownership Programs are a highly regulated structure for transferring the ownership of the company. They can also work exceptionally well for an owner's financial planning if they are executed in a manner that complies with the special tax incentives attached to the structure. While ESOPs have some tremendous benefits, they are clearly in the "Don't try this at home!" category of transfer mechanisms.

19 Leading the Team

"It's what you learn after you know it all that counts."
~ John Wooden

With your help, the client has selected the players for this game. Now what? Do you just bring them out on the field and say, "Let's go win this thing?" Of course not. Coaching may involve encouragement at times, but it's much more than that.

Every team needs a game plan. The players need to be in the right place at the right time. Someone has to be responsible for coordinating their efforts.

> **Someone has to be responsible for coordinating the team's efforts.**

The Quarterback

It's common in the Exit Planning industry for advisors to say they will "quarterback" the process. They won't. The quarterback is on the field. He takes the hits and has to make quick decisions based on what he sees. (The coach never gets sacked by a 275 lb. Defensive End!)

The quarterback of the exit planning process is the business owner. He can lose the game in a hundred ways, but he is also the only one who can win it. He can change the objectives with a single play. The rest of the team follows his direction.

The Coach

Ah finally, enter the coach. He or she is always on the sidelines. He or she plans out the game strategy, decides what resources to have available, and assigns them according to the situation.

The quarterback listens to the coach, but he is still running the team. He knows that the coach can lose the game with a bad decision, but the coach can't win the game. That only happens on the field.

The coach's job is to make the quarterback better, and to make sure that he has the proper resources available to win.

> The coach can lose the game with a bad decision, but the coach can't win the game.

The single most important talent in an exit planning team is coaching skill. Multiple technical talents are needed, from taxation to legal, financial planning, and risk management. None, however, is more important than coaching.

Put it this way. A planning team can be led from any position, as long as the person leading has coaching skills. If they don't, all the clever tax advice or ironclad legal documentation in the world won't lead to a successful transition. But if the person leading the team is an experienced coach who is dedicated to defending the owner's objectives, the outcome is far more likely to meet the owner's needs, both now and in the future.

Acknowledging Your Position
If you are going to be the coach, you'll need to make your role plain at the outset. That requires the specific acknowledgement of the client.

Often, a client will hedge when it comes to differences between two advisors. This is particularly an issue when you are newly hired, and there is resentment from a legacy advisor.

Early in my exit planning career I did an initial plan for a client who wanted to exit in three years. When I wrote it up, his CPA looked it over and said, "I can do all of this for you in the normal course of our business. You don't need another consultant to put this together for you."

The client informed me that he would be implementing the plan with his CPA. When I last spoke to him, it was seven years later and he still hadn't executed his plan.

I still feel guilty for not being experienced enough to explain to him why that was a bad idea.

In most of our engagements, other professionals typically first hear about our work when they receive a letter from the client. It is on his or her letterhead, and over the client's signature. We (of course) provide the bulk of the content. It can vary in tone and style, but it always contains several key points.

- I (the client) have chosen John to lead my transition effort.
- He will be the advisor most fully informed of my goals and objectives.
- His role is to help the entire advisor team work cooperatively on those objectives.
- He will be reaching out to you during this process both for information about my business, and for your expertise in designing a plan to meet my goals.
- Please give him your full cooperation.
- If you have any questions, feel free to call me.

I may call to follow up in the next week, or not until a few months later. I always start the conversation with, "You received the letter from <Client's name> about working with me, right?" I then tell them how happy I am that we will be working together, and we discuss the areas where I feel that their expertise will be useful (and billable).

We no longer have many issues with resentful incumbents. Handled correctly, they quickly realize that my work inevitably leads to additional revenue for them.

Working with Incumbents

While they may not be (openly) resentful, the other issue when working with a client's incumbent advisors is competence. This too should be addressed with the client at the outset.

As part of our opening conversation (after I am engaged), I tell the client that I will gladly work with his current advisors if they are qualified. If they aren't, I will discuss it with the client and we will decide together how to approach it.

As mentioned previously, my happy place is when an advisor says, "This is outside my wheelhouse. I'd like to recommend someone else for the work." When they say it in front of the client, it's even better.

I'd like to say it happens every time it's needed, but that isn't the case. All too often they say, "That doesn't look very hard. I can do it." I try to avoid having to take them down in front of their client, but offline I may have to grill them on their knowledge.

If they aren't the person for the job, I go to my next level approach. I tell them that I know practitioners who are experts in the field and that they understand that if I bring them a project, it is a one-time event. They must agree not to solicit the entire client relationship, or they risk not hearing from me again.

If that isn't convincing enough, I'll need to go to the client and relate the conversation. I've found through experience that taking on the fight now is far better than suffering through an entire engagement with a team member who can't do the job.

Referral Sources and Reciprocation

Some exit planning advisors have their "A Team" of advisors, and refuse to work with anyone else. That's fine, but it isn't the way I work. I prefer expanding my network of qualified advisors, and in turn expanding my opportunity for referrals.

Of course, that becomes an issue when we discuss referrals. Those with a fixed team often have methodologies for identifying and discussing cross-pollination of their client base. I have the opposite issue. There are very few exit planning specialists. There are lots of lawyers, accountants and wealth managers. I can't reciprocate in nearly the volumes that would be required to keep everyone happy.

As the old saying goes, "You pays yer money and you takes yer chances." Either way has some advantages and disadvantages. It's your call how to structure your teaming arrangements.

Referral Fees

We include the following language in every Phase One proposal.

> *As with any services needed through this project, we are happy to work with your current professional advisors if they are qualified. If you do not have an advisor in a specific area, we will provide several recommendations. We do not accept referral fees from other planning professionals. Any such services will be contracted directly with you.*

If the owner's strategy calls for a third-party sale, we may refer the client to a business broker or investment banker for listing and transaction representation. In such cases we feel that we've done a substantial amount of the up-front work defining cash flow, differentiation, management capabilities and other factors affecting salability. In those situations, and only with the client's permission, we will negotiate participation in the intermediaries' success fees.

20. Stakeholders

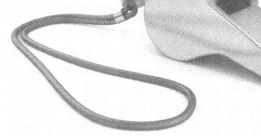

"All coaching is, is taking a player where he can't take himself."
~ Bill McCartney

Other Stakeholders

In every company there are stakeholders who are owners and those who aren't.

Inside the company, partners or minority shareholders are clearly stakeholders. Employees, vendors and customers may not have ownership, but are definitely concerned with the direction and health of the enterprise.

Outside of the company, family members are clearly influential on the owner's decision making process. Customers and vendors may also have a say in how a transfer plan is structured, and in some cases may have veto power over an owner's intentions.

> There are stakeholders who are owners, and those who aren't.

Ownership

Every advisor's discovery process has to include other owners. If there are share or membership interests in anyone else's hands besides the owner's, the sooner you can define the relationships and the authority that goes with them, the more solid your basis for planning will be.

A *Corporation* has shareholders and a Board of Directors. The Board appoints officers to handle the day-to-day business of the corporation. While governance can sometimes vary, generally speaking, the shareholders vote for Directors in proportion to their share ownership.

Partners: The term partner is frequently misused. Often minority shareholders or members of an LLC will refer to themselves as "partners," but that term really only applies to organizations filing tax returns using IRS form 1065 (U.S. Return of Partnership Income).

General Partnerships share income and liability equally between all partners. Each has an equal vote on decisions for the organization. General partnerships should not be confused with the term General Partner as described below. In a general partnership, the advisor should assume that every owner needs to be included in every step of the planning process.

Limited Partnerships have governing documents that limit both the decision-making authority and the liability of the Limited Partners. A General Partner is empowered with most decision-making authority. The Limited Partners may or may not have a right of approval on certain major decisions and may or may not have the right to remove or change the General Partner. They cannot be subjected to a capital call (a demand by the company to contribute additional funds, which can and does happen in a General Partnership).

The *General Partner* of a Limited Partnership may be an individual, a corporation or a Limited Liability Company (LLC). This is where the decision making power resides. If it is a corporation or an LLC, the shareholders or members may be a single individual, a select group of Limited Partners, or all of the Limited Partners.

Limited Liability Companies are a more flexible form of business entity that has become widely popular over the last few decades. An LLC has Members. Much like shareholders or Limited Partners, those Members appoint Managers, who serve in a similar capacity to a Board of Directors in a Corporation.

The flexibility of an LLC lies in two areas. First, while an LLC offers liability protection similar to a Corporation or a Limited Partnership, it is not recognized as a distinct type of entity by the Internal Revenue Service. The LLC has to choose between filing a corporate tax return (IRS 1120 or 1120-S) and a partnership return. From a Federal standpoint, it is treated according to the type of filing it chooses.

The second feature of an LLC is that it can draft governing rules that permit distributions of income that are asynchronous to ownership. Instead of allocating distributions by numbers of shares or profits by partnership interests, it can choose to pay out "profit interests" using any formula the members choose.

This isn't intended to be an exhaustive description of business entities. What I am pointing out, however, is the importance of understanding the kind of entity or entities you are dealing with as an advisor. That's why every engagement should begin with a review of the formation documents.

> Every engagement should begin with a review of the formation documents.

Whether those documents include articles of incorporation, shareholder or member agreements, a buy/sell agreement or other documentation, you wouldn't be the first advisor to discover that the decision-making authority a client claims is not really as represented. Just as in valuations or the selection of advisors, you can't assume that an owner knows the rules and restrictions of his or her entity.

For example, I recently had a third-generation owner tell me that only he, of all the family members, had voting shares in the corporation. A quick review showed that he held the majority of shares (but all shares voted) in the General Partner of a Limited Partnership where the partnership interests were controlled inside a trust. From a practical operating perspective, he had the authority to make all the decisions. From a transfer perspective, that was anything but the case.

Other Internal Stakeholders

Phantom owners are shareholders or members who have left the business. Perhaps they sold their ownership. Sometimes their departure from active participation in the business disqualifies them from ownership. In other cases their holdings were formally redeemed, but the governing documents were never updated, or the stock certificates were never returned.

Your initial review of the documentation should encompass a review for phantom owners. Clearing up any historical "hanging chads" can save you a lot of headaches and your client considerable expense down the road.

> **Initial review of documentation should encompass a review for phantom owners.**

Employees are the other internal stake-holders in any organization. While our exit planning engagements are focused on the principal owner or owners, the impact on employees has to be considered in light of a few questions.

Are they critical to business operations? Every organization has key employees, but "key" and "irreplaceable" are two different things. Each key employee should be assessed to determine whether their opposition could derail a transition plan.

Are they a flight risk? If the departure of an employee could threaten the survivability of the company, they will have to be secured by stay agreements or participation in the sale proceeds.

Do they expect ownership? Over the course of years, owners say lots of things to employees. "You think and act like an owner." "I consider you my partner." "All this could be yours someday." and of course "I'm going to sell (or give) you ownership." All of these are examples of casual comments that may have been said a long time ago. The owner may have meant it differently, forgotten he said it, or subsequently changed his opinion of the employee.

It doesn't matter. If the employee is working under the impression that he or she has ownership, is supposed to get it, or is otherwise entitled to ownership-level participation, the advisor has to know it at the outset.

External Stakeholders

Family is the most obvious external influence on any plan. Although it seems elementary, an advisor should first learn whether the owner has even discussed transition with their family.

"Honey, I sold the company!" may not be as warmly received as they imagined.

Customers are a critical factor in any ownership transition as well. In the case of written purchase contracts, there may be a right to rebid or cancel upon a change of control. This is especially common in agreements with government entities of publicly traded corporations.

> "Honey, I sold the company!" may not be as warmly received as they imagined.

Even if there are no such conditions, a transition plan should carefully consider the impact on customers, and the possibility that they may see any uncertainty as a reason to seek another supplier.

Vendors are rarely an issue, but they can create some. Usually, they are as happy to sell to a new owner as they were to the old one. In cases where there are exclusive distribution rights, however, you may see change of control provisions similar to those in customer contracts.

Don't Tell Anyone!

Many owners are afraid that the knowledge that they are planning an exit will create company-threatening responses from stakeholders.

For that reason, there is an order to sharing the information that can be used as a general guideline.

Family first. If the idea of transitioning hasn't been communicated to the immediate family, it should be. In some cases, the family may be owners or employed in the business. Family owners are definitely in the first tier of communication. A family member employee may be brought in early or not, depending on maturity and their expectations for the future.

Employees are usually the ones whom owners want to keep in the dark as long as possible. Ideally, they have been exposed to the idea of a transition long before planning even begins. I've worked with many owners who started a decade or more before their anticipated sale with comments like, "You wouldn't want to work in a company that wasn't looking out for your future, right?" and "We all know that I'm not going to be running this business forever." (Of course, make sure those kinds of comments were not and are not perceived as, "*You will be running this business!*")

When there is a change of control on the table, I recommend using the concentric circle approach to information sharing with employees.

You start with your inner circle of most trusted employees. Tell them what is anticipated, but make it plain that the information is only for them. It is not to be shared until you decide to do so, but when you do, they can expect other employees to look to them for their reaction. Of course, they are then able to say, "It's ok, I already knew about it."

This approach gives recognition and status to a certain group. It can be repeated for a second circle and even a third before sharing the information publicly.

A caution. Not everyone can resist the telling eyeroll or knowing smirk when they are "hiding" secret information. Share judiciously, and don't rely on confidentiality for too long. I've used this method for a 4-circle distribution over as little as two days, and it still works really well.

Customers and vendors should be the last to know. Unless it is required as part of a buyer's due diligence, I prefer to leave the announcement until it is notice of a *fait accompli*. In most cases, inertia will come through, and business relationships will continue much as before.

21. Internal Buyers

"When I was young I used to say, treat everybody right. That's bull. Treat everybody fairly."
~ Bear Bryant

There are two kinds of internal stakeholders that can be buyers, employed family members and non-family employees.

> Family businesses are a special breed with three levels of interaction.

Family businesses are a special breed with three levels of interaction. There are multiple levels of relationships between parents, children, and siblings. There are the ownership relationships, which may include family members who have a say in the running of the business, but are not involved on a day-to-day basis.

There are the management relationships. These are created artificially by the naming of officers and assignments of responsibility. All too frequently, the management responsibilities are doled out by age, seniority, or closeness of a blood relationship. They may or may not reflect an ability to actually exercise authority within the organization.

Of course, underlying all interactions are the blood (and often marriage) relationships. Regardless of equity holdings or organizational charts, there is inevitably a bit of "I'll always be your mother," or "You're still my little brother," in every connection.

THREE-CIRCLE MODEL
OF THE FAMILY BUSINESS SYSTEM

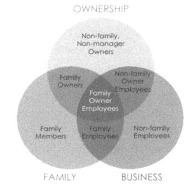

145

There is a well-known diagram of the three circles of relationships overlapping each other. Where all three share the same space in the center it can sometimes be reminiscent of the old warning on the perimeter of early Flat Earth maps, "Here, there be monsters."

Absentee Owners

The Bear Bryant quote that starts this chapter is easy to say, but much harder to practice in real life. Parents may have vastly different ideas of what fair treatment entails. When the business is the largest single asset in the family holdings, it may be difficult to assign the bulk of the value in the estate to the children who work in their business, and then leave the others out in the cold.

As an advisor, I will argue vociferously against even distribution between working and not working children. The idea that some children will work for the rest of their careers to build an organization where a substantial portion of the benefits go to siblings who had nothing to do with creating them almost inevitably leads to resentment.

I tell clients who are anticipating such a division that they may be ruining the family Thanksgiving for the rest of their lives. Often that imagery gets them to reconsider.

Nonetheless when such division is an established fact or is passionately desired by the parents, I try to find a way to be both fair and equitable. Typically, we will agree to such a division upon the death of the parents or a scheduled transfer event. We will have the noninvolved children enter into a binding agreement to sell their shares to the working children at that time. The value is set by a formula, and the transfer of ownership is simultaneous with their receipt of same.

This allows the children who aren't in the business to realize the full value of what the parents have built until such time as they step away from the company. The inheritors of the business pay their siblings a fair price for the value at that point, and enjoy 100% of any increase or decrease in the value under their management.

There are a number of different studies about the likelihood of a family business surviving through generations. In most, the percentage of a successful transfer past the third generation is 3% or less.[15] I think this number could be dramatically improved with fair transition planning.

I know in a number of cases where ownership continued to be diluted through successive generations, the reason the business passed out of the family's hands was because the operating member has such a small percentage of ownership that it was no longer worth it for him or her to carry the burden of paying everyone else.

It is important to remember that there are a number of family business psychologists and consultants who specialize in "family governance." These practitioners specialize in family constitutions, structures that document decision making processes for when there are disagreements. Do not hesitate to include one of them on the team.

Selling to Employees

As I stated earlier, when we ask, "Do you have employees who can run this business?" the answer is frequently, "Yes, but they have no money to buy it."

That's not really an obstacle and is actually relatively easy to fix, but it requires time. In a business with reasonable cash flow, we can usually design a transfer in three or four years. Five to eight years is ideal. I learned this methodology from John Brown, the founder of the Business Enterprise Institute, in my first BEI Boot Camp. As soon as I saw it illustrated on a white board, I knew my days as a business broker were limited.

> The owner can control the time, method and proceeds of the sale.

Simply put, the owner sells stock to employees for a note. After a few years, the employees control a minority interest, some of which has been paid and some of which is still subject to a promissory note. The owner can then subordinate the note balance to an SBA (or commercial) loan for the balance of the equity.

Done correctly, the owner can walk away with 80% or more of the purchase price in cash.

He or she controls the time, method and proceeds of the sale. There is no dickering over price, much less exhaustive due diligence, and the employees are highly motivated to continue making the company even more successful.

This kind of transfer requires an understanding of two concepts. First, the cash flow of the company is the only means of financing a purchase. Second, time and risk are counterforces in the transaction structure.

Company Cash Flow
We begin by examining the free cash flow of the business. By that I mean the amount the client feels he can use for the transfer apart from what he wants for his own living expenses.

The cash flow of the business is always the only means to pay for a transfer. If a buyer pays all cash, the cash flow represents his return on investment. If the deal is financed, it is the only means to repay the loan.

In an internal transfer, cash distributions to the employees are their only means of paying a promissory note. It involves double taxation on the employees' distributions and when the remaining proceeds are paid to the seller, but there are structural methods that can be used to reduce that burden.

Few internal transfers can realize a higher price than a negotiated sale to a third party.

The owner has to understand that he is giving up some cash flow now, so that he can control the entire transaction event. He also has to want the employees to have ownership.

The employee buyers, on the other hand, must realize that they are essentially getting the opportunity to buy the company for free. Note that I said "opportunity." Giving them the money to make a down payment, even if it is conditioned on performance, is still funding their first step.

They need to realize that opportunity is coming out of the owner's pocket. He is foregoing better personal income now so that he can control the variables. Believe me, every owner (*every one*) mentions that the employees are buying the business with *his* cash flow.

We typically let the price of equity float with the financial results of the business. That means if they help the business have a successful year, their purchases are at a higher value. This inevitably leads to the complaint (every time) that they are acting against their own interests. I always bring this to their attention at the very beginning of any explanations. As I tell them, "True, but it isn't your money to start with."

Finally, the employees must understand that their risk-free ownership comes to a halt in a specific time frame. When the owner leaves, it will be because they have taken on sufficient debt to close the deal. There is a date, and an estimated amount they will need. It will be their job to qualify for the loan, and to guaranty it.

> The employee's risk-free ownership comes to a halt in a specific time frame.

Time vs. Risk

Occasionally an owner will ask me "What is the fastest you can sell my company?" My response is "I can do it in about a week."

That's how long it will take to have an attorney draft a sale agreement and a promissory note for 100% of the purchase price. The employee or employees sign the note and presto! The business is sold.

Of course, the risk is extreme. The employees are untrained, and very likely unqualified. The odds of receiving full payment on the note are pretty slim, but it *is* undeniably fast.

From that time frame forward, every added year reduces the risk. In an employee or family sale, there is time for training, arranging third party financing and a rational hand off of duties. Sale structures can reward the buyers for growing the business, and, not incidentally, for eventually paying the seller more than it is worth today.

If the strategy is a sale to a third party, there is time to develop clean due diligence information, get stay agreements with key employees and put together a qualified deal team.

The equation is simple. More time equals less risk. In an eight to ten year plan, we can frequently have owners leave with more than they might realize today, and with 100% of the proceeds in hand.

22 You Can't Aways Get What You Want

"You can't always get what you want, but if you try sometimes, you'll find, you get what you need."

~ Mick Jagger

Expectations

The Pepperdine Capital Markets Survey reports that intermediaries (Brokers, investment bankers and private equity groups) indicate that the #1 reason for the failure to sell a company is "the seller's unrealistic expectations of price."

> The #1 reason for the failure to sell a company is "the seller's unrealistic expectations of price."

As mentioned earlier, a substantial plurality of exit planning professionals blame "insufficient proceeds" as the reason 75% of sellers are unhappy or have "profound regrets" a year after selling their businesses.

Are owner's suffering from widespread delusions, or are advisors succumbing to the "It's not my fault!" excuse?

It's probably a little of both. Every advisor has experience with owners who have unrealistic ideas about the value of their business, but I find it difficult to believe that, given the length and complexity of the average sale transaction, they are shocked by the price they agreed to. From initial offers to letters of intent, through the representations and warrantees in a purchase agreement, to quality of earnings audits and due diligence, a seller has plenty of time to understand the market value of their business.

Of course, some seller's remorse is to be expected. No matter how long or arduous the negotiation process, the seller will always wonder whether he could have gotten just a little more for the business. But it's difficult to believe that falling a bit short on price would lead to "profound regret" a year later. I don't know many owners who are that OCD.

So, we return to our initial argument. Exited owners are unhappy because they don't have activity, identity and purpose to fill the void left when they move to their Second Act.

Who is Responsible?
I realize that I'm harping on this point. This is where the exit planning coach has the most important role as a truth-sayer. No one else takes on the responsibility of a happy client a year down the road.

> No one else takes on the responsibility of a happy client a year down the road.

The CPA is charged with structuring a tax-efficient transaction, not ensuring a happy client.

The attorney is charged with representing the client's interests and controlling liabilities, not worrying about his next life as a former owner.

The broker or other intermediary is charged with finding a qualified buyer and bringing him to the deal. His responsibility ends on the day the deal closes.

The estate planning attorney and the wealth manager are responsible for protecting the proceeds. Their jobs begin only after the transaction.

When you accept the role of coach, you are taking on the duty of the client's satisfaction a year down the road. It may require some difficult conversations.

Reality Bites
Reading this book may help you to dig deeper into a client's plans for life after the business. The one thing it cannot teach is tenacity.

By now I hope every reader understands that the conversation has to go beyond, "I'll play a lot of golf." Getting a business owner to really, really commit to a plan beyond the company usually requires asking questions again, and again, and again.

Playing a lot of golf becomes,

Playing a lot of golf and fishing on my new boat. (Sorry, we aren't close to reaching your 50 hour a week activity level yet,) so it becomes,

Playing a lot of golf and fishing on my new boat and visiting with my grandchildren. (OK, a few more hours a week, but your kids probably don't need or want co-parents) so it becomes,

Playing a lot of golf and fishing and grandchildren and working in my church. (What will you be doing for the church? How much time will it take?)

Playing golf and fishing and grandchildren and serving meals in the church senior center. (Good for our purpose, but how does a task-based job address your identity?)

Playing golf and fishing and grandchildren and running the church's senior center.

Sounds like a lot? If you are being diligent about the vision, you are probably still short at least 20 hours a week. Purpose is being addressed, but unless the client plans on getting business cards that say "Head of the Church's Senior Kitchen" he is probably still well short of the identity requirement.

> Clients don't want to examine their future that closely.

It's not easy. Clients don't want to examine their future that closely. They may grow more resistant as you keep asking for more.

If it was easy...
everyone would be doing it.

153

23 The Dismal Ds:
Contingency & Continuity Planning

"You have no choices about how you lose, but you do have a choice about how you come back and prepare to win again."

~ Pat Riley

The "Dismal Ds" are dark humor in exit planning. Every industry and profession has something of the type. In some, it's "You can have it done well, done fast, or done cheaply. Pick any two." In planning it's "Sooner or later, every owner exits his or her business... 100% guaranteed."

> "Sooner or later, every owner exits his or her business... 100% guaranteed."

Clearly, this refers to the unplanned but inevitable departure from the biggest D - Death. That isn't the only D, however. There are others, NONE of which lead to a controlled, lucrative, or enjoyable transition. Most start with dis- defined as "dis-", a Latin prefix meaning "apart," "asunder," "away," "utterly," or having a privative, negative, or reversing force."

All of those applications fit multiple Ds.

Besides Death, the other Dismal Ds include:

- **Disease** - The critical illness of the owner or an irreplaceable employee.
- **Dissension** - between partners, shareholders, or family members.
- **Disaster** - Fire, flood, storm, or accident.

- **Disability** - An owner's inability to oversee operations.
- **Disinterest** - Of the founder or next-generation ownership.
- **Distraction** - When an owner's focus is elsewhere, (frequently love or owning a bar.)
- **Disarray** - More simply, bad management.
- **Dishonesty** - Financial fraud or other skullduggery.
- **Disenchantment** - A fancy word for burnout.
- **Divorce** - A bitter personal fight over the business assets, ownership, or value.
- **Debt** - Leverage taken on in good times but no longer sustainable.
- **Depression** - Economic malaise (think hospitality businesses in 2020.)
- **Defection**- The poaching or bolting of a key employee, frequently in sales.
- **Defenestration** - Getting fatally thrown from a window.

(Okay, I may have gone too far with that last one, but I couldn't resist. We don't see it much in practice.)

Planning - The Cure for the Dismal Ds

The point is, there are many ways to a forced exit from a business due to circumstances. Some might be beyond a client's control, but most can be avoided.

- **Disease** - Have solid business continuity instructions in place.
- **Dissension** - Start with a good buy/sell or shareholders' agreement that makes it plain how disagreements will be handled.

- **Disaster** - Fire, flood, storm, or accidents can be insured, including loss of revenue.
- **Disability** - Again, have solid business continuity instructions in place.
- **Disinterest** - Start implementing an exit plan before the business suffers the effects. In brokerage, we used to say, "Show me an owner who says he is burned out, and I'll show you financial statements that evidenced the problem three years ago."
- **Distraction** - Don't let your client buy a bar. Don't let them buy another business. Don't let them have an affair.
- **Disarray** - Get the client to accept some outside help. Consulting, coaching and peer groups all work well.
- **Dishonesty** - Have an outside party check the company's systems and security regularly.
- **Disenchantment** - Again, start implementing an exit plan before the business suffers the effects.
- **Divorce -** Help the client settle the value of the business first, preferably before the lawyers do it.
- **Debt** - Limit debt to half of what the current cash flow can service.
- **Depression** - If a client has to cut expenses, help him do so deeply and quickly.
- **Defection** - Two words, employment agreements.
- **Defenestration** - Stay away from the Departed, or Irish, Italian, and Jewish mobsters in general. Alternatively, live and work where there are only single-story buildings.

I obviously have my tongue firmly planted in my cheek with a few of these, but my point should be clear. Your client's business is probably the most valuable asset in their life. Losing it to unplanned events hurts. Even if the owner is no longer in the picture, there is a huge impact on family, employees and customers.

A good exit plan, whether it's in place for implementation now or years down the road, should take many, if not all of the Dismal Ds into account. All entrepreneurs want control over their future. That is why they are entrepreneurs. Planning isn't merely an intellectual exercise. It's all about control.

Some of "Da D's" are just typical reasons behind putting a business up for sale. They include Dissension among partners, Declining sales, Divorce, Disinterest, Distraction of the owner and Debt.

Others are the driving force for an emergency sale, usually far below the fair market value. Those are Disaster, Disease, Disability and Death. If you wait long enough, one of these four horsemen of business apocalypse will claim your transition.

> If you wait long enough, one of these four horsemen of the business apocalypse will claim your transition.

Business Continuity Instructions

In every exit plan we do there are Business Continuity Instructions. As I instruct our Affiliates around the country, BCIs should be part of every engagement. Only a small percentage of our clients will need them, but for those who do, they will be the most important and valuable part of our services.

There are two types of planning tools that often go by the name BCI, but fall short in my opinion, by neglecting some key areas of preparation. One is risk planning usually associated with insurance. These are questionnaires that focus on financial risk management. Do you have sufficient policy benefits to take care of the business and your family? Do you have an income source to supplement your family's expenses if your paycheck stops?

The other is business interruption planning, usually in anticipation of a natural disaster. Do you have backup records, a place to establish phone answering, and alternative communication channels with your employees? This is contingency planning.

Contingency vs. Continuity Planning

When advisors talk about preparing for unforeseen problems, they frequently commingle the terms contingency and continuity. The terms are not synonymous, and there are important differences between them.

> Contingency planning is generally accepted to mean how a business will respond in the event of a disaster.

Contingency planning is generally accepted to mean how a business will respond in the event of a disaster. This could entail a building fire, severe weather, a strike of key service workers, civil unrest or riots (depending on the audience.) In this age of cybersecurity, ransomware or a denial of service attack, identity theft and electronic fraud are all well qualified to be categorized as disasters as well.

Generally speaking, these are all insurable events, and contingency planning often recommends insurance as a major component of preparedness, along with remote working capabilities or alternative production resources. In privately held businesses, however, contingency planning has one weakness.

It assumes that the owner of the company will be available to oversee the implementation of the plan.

Continuity Planning

Both financial risk assessment and disaster contingency scenarios are useful, but neither takes the more operational approach that we do. Our BCI starts with one simple question. **"What happens if you are suddenly and unexpectedly absent from your business for an indefinite time?"**

We begin from day one, hour one. How does the business open and function? Who is responsible for telling the employees? The vendors?

The customers? Who has access to the bank accounts? Where are spare keys and security codes? Most importantly, who has the authority to make immediate decisions regarding operations, finance, personnel and administration?

Who are your key advisors? Who should be contacted regarding legal, accounting, insurance, leasehold or benefit issues? Are there other trusted advisors who should be included on major decisions? What authority do they have?

Is your Board of Directors capable of guiding the company? We find many smaller corporations where the owner is the only officer and Director. That means in his or her absence the company is incapable of functioning legally. Who names replacement officers?

New directors must be elected by shareholders. In the event of an owner's death, ownership of the business may go into probate, crippling its ability to function.

Exit Planning is presumably designed around a voluntary departure from the business, but what if it isn't voluntary? Where Contingency planning looks at a variety of financial risks, Continuity planning is focused on the operational problems of an owner's absence.

Continuity planning begins with the operational aspects of running the business, but it continues through a variety of related issues.

> Continuity planning begins with the operational aspects of running the business.

Buy/Sell or Shareholder Agreements

Many Contingency plans call for funding equity buyouts using insurance in the event of a stockholder's death. Disability, however, is often ignored or assumed. Most such agreements call for a buyout in the event of "death or disability" but the funding mechanism of an insurance policy is silent on the issue of disability. Unless a second policy is in place, all of the documentation describing how ownership transfers may be moot.

One area where we see frequent issues involves life insurance on the owner. If it is intended to purchase the stock from family members, who is the buyer? A company cannot buy itself. There has to be at least one other owner to execute the purchase. We have run into insurance-funded buy/sell agreements where one of the partners retired years ago. There is no one left to be the buyer in the event of the remaining partner's demise.

If the proceeds of insurance are intended to provide working capital, are they also pledged to the bank for a credit line? Do the policies have restrictions on their distribution?

A particularly ugly scenario is where owners have a buy/sell agreement funded by life insurance. In order to make the premiums tax deductible, they choose to have the company pay the premiums. The benefit is paid to the company with the intention of buying out the surviving family. However, the company is already in dire straits without its majority owner, and the remaining shareholder(s) hold onto the cash, leaving the deceased owner's family without income while they litigate.

If a key owner is gone, there might be issues with credit and banking facilities. What safeties are in place to prevent the proceeds from being used to cover working capital or other company expenses instead of paying them to family survivors? Unless you have conditions in the insurance agreement restricting payouts, the only way a client's family can access the benefits is to sue the company.

> If a key owner is gone, there might be issues with credit and banking facilities.

Even when insurance is in place, its benefit is frequently short of the current fair market value of the business. Does the buy/sell have a reasonable approach for valuing the business? If the value is in excess of the policy benefit, what contingent payment mechanisms are defined for an alternative buyout? Are there limits on the amount of cash flow that can be committed to one or more buyouts?

If another shareholder decides that he or she doesn't want to be an owner in the absence of the deceased/disabled owner, are the rights of sale the same for the second buyout?

Trusted Advisors
Who should the family or the employees go to for advice on decisions? As with trusted employees, many owners presume that long-time advisors will be willing to help. Also, like employees, advisors have an indeterminate time limit on how long or how much they might be willing to donate.

As a trusted advisor, you are likely to be among those named for helping the family or employees. Think about it from your own admittedly selfish point of view. What would be your concerns? Are you in a position to "jump in" without notice? What advice are you qualified to give? What decisions are you qualified to make?

A client once told me that he had written a letter to his daughters titled, "If the plane goes down." In it he told them to make no decisions about his $50,000,000 company without consulting me. Although I was flattered, the questions above ran through my head. Am I supposed to take over the CEO position in that company? It certainly sounded like a full-time position. Is there compensation involved?

When you are helping an owner create a contingency plan, the role of advisors and their limitations should be included. Most importantly, define the hierarchy of decision making. Are the advisors limited to advising, or are they expected to take a more active role? If it's the latter, what are the terms?

> The role of advisors and their limitations should be included in the contingency plan.

The good news is that creating a continuity plan is an excellent way to develop action steps for exit planning. You will naturally develop a better idea of where the company is prepared for the owner to move on, and where lack of preparation is an obstacle to an orderly exit.

Employee Compensation and Stay Bonuses

Continuity also requires that the company retain key employees. Like advisors, they are likely expected to increase their responsibility. Most long-term employees will happily step up to help out. If their duties are greatly expanded, it won't be too long before they start wondering about additional compensation.

> Continuity also requires that the company retain key employees.

If employees are expected to step up to a higher level of responsibility, is there contingent compensation attached to the added responsibility? Many owners rightfully anticipate that employees will shoulder additional duties out of loyalty, but loyalty has a limit. What if they are in this position for months?

Are there parameters on the employees' decision-making authority? Can they make the decisions on new capital investments, or enter into new vendor relationships? If there is a dollar limit, who has the authority to exceed it, if necessary? Who are the key advisors they should consult if they have questions? Is there a compensation agreement with those advisors if they need to be closely involved or engaged for an extended time period?

Does their authority extend to selling the company?

Are key employees a flight risk? If they have to step up to a level beyond their normal responsibilities, will their compensation reflect their new authority? Who decides what they are worth?

Consider attaching separate compensation instructions to "interim" titles for key employees and include compensation to match the responsibilities. If the event causing an owner's absence is temporary, the employee will understand that the title and pay are as well. If it is permanent, the company will have a defined management structure until other steps can be taken.

If the plan calls for the sale or liquidation of the business in the absence of the owner, there is even more reason to address employee compensation as part of the plan. In many cases, the top employees may be negotiating for the elimination of their own positions.

In such cases, stay bonuses can preserve the operating structure until a sale is executed. Ideally, such a bonus would be structured with a guarantee (placed in escrow from the sale proceeds) of a percentage of the employee's salary for staying through the transition. It should also include a second bonus based on achieving a reasonable minimum target price.

Working Capital and Credit Guarantees

The finances of a company that is missing its leader are components of both Contingency and Continuity planning. Since they are primarily financial risks, they can be insured. As mentioned previously, however, any insurance policy should be structured to function in the absence of the owner.

I once interviewed ten different banking executives about personal guarantees. I asked whether that meant they immediately and automatically swept all operating accounts of the business as soon as they learned about an owner's death. They said that they did.

I asked whether that could mean that the company failed, employees were unpaid, and the family of the owner was left with no income. Not only did they agree that such was the case, but *every one* of them then told me a story about a personal experience where exactly that happened to a client. Each also went to some length to express how badly he felt about it.

> Contingency planning should include the purchase of insurance to secure sufficient working capital.

Contingency planning should include the purchase of insurance to secure sufficient working capital for the company to continue, or if necessary to pay off a credit line. Such insurance should also provide for a funded buy/sell agreement or continuing income for the owner's family.

Continuity planning should include informing the lenders of the existence of such security. As my conversations with the banking executives showed, the bank will act to secure its own interest first and worry about the damage later. There needs to be an understanding, preferably written, describing the bank's willingness to wait for their security to be perfected.

> Continuity planning should include informing the lenders of the existence of such security

Licenses

In many smaller professional or trade businesses where licensing is a prerequisite, the owner is often the sole licensee. The absence of a license can render the firm dead in the water.

Continuity planning should include an arrangement with a friend or even a friendly competitor or other for "borrowing" their signature on items requiring a license. It should also specify the compensation for this service.

24. Life After the Business

> *"The key is not the will to win. Everybody has that. It's the will to prepare to win that is important."*
> ~ Bobby Knight

I started this book by describing our mission. We want business owners to be happy with the result of their transitions. For that to happen, they have to develop, understand and gladly anticipate three things.

Purpose – The feeling that what they are doing is important, or at least important to them.

Identity – When Bob is no longer "Bob of Bob's Widget's," who is he?

Activity – Very simply, filling in the day with something other than television.

Although we discussed them previously in Chapters 15 and 22, it is important enough to visit again before we are done.

Entrepreneurs Don't Have Rearview Mirrors

All business owners are goal-oriented. From the day they founded or assumed control of their company, they have set targets and achieved them. That is why they are successful. They know how to define a goal and make it happen.

If you ask them to tell you about the best thing that they did in the business three years ago, they will respond with, "I have no idea." or "Why would I know that?" or "Why is that important?" They can't tell you because it happened in the past and they cannot focus on a target that's behind them. In fact, they can't see it at all. They are too busy looking forward.

I've even had some owners get angry. They feel that they should be able to tell me, and that they are somehow failing a test if they don't. The fact is, no entrepreneur has ever been able to give me a cogent answer about accomplishments in the past.

If you ask, "What do you plan to do in the coming year?" they will give you a flood of responses. There are plans to increase sales, hire new employees, or enter into a new area of business. Whether or not they have a formal strategic planning process, they inevitably have a pretty good idea of the changes and improvements they want to implement in their company for the future.

Visioning the Future
An entrepreneur's vision of "What's next?" is frequently the most neglected aspect of their exit planning. They may term their goals for exiting in measurable, concrete terms. "I want to retire in five years with ten million dollars in the bank," is an archetypical example. Others will couch their vision in terms of people. "I want financial security for my family, and continuing employment for my staff."

All too often, their vision for the future deemphasizes or completely neglects their own individual needs. As described previously, when pressed to enunciate more personal goals, they'll often respond with something like, "I guess I'll just play a lot of golf."

You heard it here, "Playing a lot of golf is not a retirement plan."

In a recent survey from PwC, they reported that 75% of business owners have regrets a year after they leave the business. The Exit Planning Institute did a survey ten years ago with the same result. According to Riley Moines, author of *The Ten Lessons: How You Too Can Squeeze All The "Juice" Out of Retirement*, six months to a year is the typical initial "vacation" period when the retiree catches up on travel and recreational activities.

After that first year, the reason so many ex-owners are unhappy is because they didn't have a clear vision for their life after the business. Their expectations simply did not take into account the reality of what would happen when they were no longer spending the majority of their time working.

Leaping into the Void
When I ask about their plans for the next year, some owners are more specific than others. But none of them ever say, "I don't know. We may make money, or we may lose money. We may grow, or we may shrink. Whatever happens, happens. It doesn't matter."

Why do advisors expect that someone who has driven towards goals for their whole life will suddenly be happy without purpose, without identity, and without a plan? It isn't surprising that so many owners are reluctant to discuss exit planning at all. Life without the daily challenges and decisions that come with running a business seems unattractive. Their vision of the future is a void.

> Life without the daily challenges and decisions that come with running a business seems unattractive.

The success of an exit strategy depends less on the amount of money the transfer generates than it does on the personal satisfaction of the client. Unless you can help an entrepreneur identify a vision for a "next act" that is more appealing than the current one, they won't be anxious to move towards it.

Purpose
In Bob Buford's classic book *Halftime*, he does an excellent job of discussing the importance of purpose after exiting. He makes several great points that form the foundation of my discussions on the topic with owners. These may not be the way he portrays them in the book, but it is how my thinking was affected by it.

If they really love it, they are likely doing it already. A claim by an owner that they will engage in an entirely new cause because they have merely been "too busy" to do anything in that area before is most likely bogus. I know very busy owners who created the time to dig water wells in Central America, sponsor orphanages, or build medical clinics in Africa. Part of their plan after exiting was to do *more* to support such efforts, but they already knew it was what they wanted to do, and had experienced it.

Do what they are good at, not just what an organization needs. Our clients have built successful companies. They may support a cause that seeks extra hands ladling beans in a soup kitchen or installing windows. That may be fun once in a while, but they won't be happy working that far below their "pay grade" for long. Help clients identify organizations that are willing to recognize their special skill set, appreciate it and can take advantage of it.

Avoid locking into time commitments. It's easy to promise help every Tuesday or attending every monthly Board meeting, but the owner didn't go through a transition from the business just so he or she could take on a new job. Help them examine their options in light of their new-found freedom. They may not be accustomed to having this much flexibility, but they shouldn't give it up until they are really sure they are ready to.

Identity

This area may be beyond the scope of most exit planning advisors, but "Who am I?" is a critical piece in the post-exit puzzle.

For some owners, a perfectly acceptable answer to that question is "Grandpa," but it isn't enough for most. I've frequently heard (and so have you), "The best thing about grandchildren is that they go home."

As petty as it seems, titles are important. Business owners have 30, 40 or 50 years of experience telling people, "I am the owner of…" or "I am the president of…" They have business cards that proclaim their importance.

I recently interviewed an owner who sits on ten different Boards. It would be hard to look at his resume without recognizing at least a few of the organizations. They range from a bank to a national sports organization and encompass several professional, trade and educational relationships. He will not only retire with an identity, but he even has different identities for different situations.

> Exiting owners should begin defining their post-ownership relationships well before their departure date.

Exiting owners should begin defining their post-ownership relationships well before their departure date. Sitting on a Board, teaching, or consulting all bring legitimate titles with positions. Work with clients on what their new business card or email signature will say after they have transitioned.

Activity

In chapter 15, we discussed the nuts and bolts of our ExitMap® exercise on time. I return to the result throughout an engagement. The other day, I was discussing an operations issue with a planning client. Before I got off the phone I asked him "How are you doing with those 19.8 hours a week you still have to fill?"

The surveys of owners that show dissatisfaction don't dive more deeply into the reasons, but one is certainly boredom. Anecdotally, I can tell many stories of successfully transitioned owners who bought another business just to have "something to do."

Thankfully, most purchased a smaller business that didn't risk their entire capital. In almost every instance they wound up selling or closing it within a year or two. In one case however, the client purchased a business for his daughter to run, and together they built it larger than his original company.

Regardless of the anecdotes, I want to finish this dissertation on coaching by emphasizing the importance of discussing purpose, identity and activity with every exit planning client. You may not be able to help them reach a specific financial goal, but if you help them grasp a vision for life after the business, you've performed a great service.

Thank You

This brings to a close our discussion. I grew to visualize you, the reader, quite clearly. It's not a photo image, so details of size, age and gender are nebulous.

What comes through clearly is someone who wants to be the most trusted advisor. Who wants their clients to move on to a Second Act as something even more rewarding than the first.

I hope this came through to you as a conversation. Not like sitting in a classroom. More like sitting in a lounge over a drink. We trade war stories and we each learn something. It's also the oldest form of education in the world.

Thanks for listening.

THE COACHING DISCOVERY DELIVERABLE

The output of the approach and the process is the deliverable, what you give to the clients. It's your carefully built and organized plan for the most important financial event of their lives.

That Coaching Discovery deliverable should have several attributes:

It has helped the business owner develop a vision attractive enough to fully replace their business. The owner has considered activity, identity and purpose after the exit, and has developed an "entry plan" for life after the company.

It has tested the owner's objectives and recommended how to either reach the goals or modify them. It should be professional, but a bit painful if necessary.

It has fully educated the client on the options available, and provided insight to help them through the decision process.

It has prepared the owner to take the next steps.

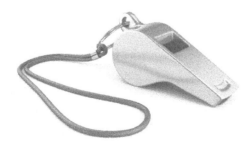

AFTERWARD:
Main Street or Middle-Market?

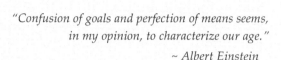

> *"Confusion of goals and perfection of means seems, in my opinion, to characterize our age."*
> ~ Albert Einstein

A common area of confusion among advisors is the difference between a "Main Street" business, a "Middle Market" business and a "Mom and Pop" business. While strictly speaking it isn't a coaching skill, it is something that we run into frequently. I thought I'd share my research and ideas about it.

Main Street Businesses

The term Main Street is defined by the International Business Brokers' Association and other professional intermediary organizations as any company with a Fair Market Value of less than $3,000,000. That is about the upper limit of a business that can be purchased by an individual using "normal" 20% down financing. They are acquiring for the purpose of earning a living.

Main Street businesses typically calculate cash flow as Seller's Discretionary Earnings (SDE). As discussed by Scott Gabehart, the creator of BizEquity valuation software, SDE is a better measure of a business's return on owner labor, rather than return on investment. SDE includes the benefits of ownership including salary, employer taxes, distributions, health insurance, vehicle and other perks of ownership. It also includes non-cash tax deductions such as depreciation.

The average selling price for an owner-operated business in the United States is 2.3 times its SDE. That cash flow has to support any debt as well as provide a living for the principal operator.

My own experience in representing owners, along with sources like BizEquity, find that multiple to be accurate. So we can safely say that the common definition of "Main Street" encompasses businesses that produce up to $1.3 million in cash flow. That number is actually pretty high, and crosses the threshold of where Private Equity companies often seek acquisitions. At that level an entrepreneurial buyer would need $600,000 for a down payment and about $25,000 a month for debt service. That is beyond the capabilities of most individuals.

In reality, companies that generate more than $500,000 a year in adjusted EBITDA cash flow (not counting owner compensation) are more commonly sold for multiples of EBITDA. At that size, a multiple of four times adjusted cash flow is pretty common, and could classify a company with up to about $750,000 in adjusted cash flow as "Main Street."

Mom and Pop Businesses
There is no definition of what is too small to be considered "Main Street," but I like the description used by Doug Tatum, author of *No Man's Land: Where Growing Companies Fail*. Doug says that many entrepreneurs start a company to build wealth. They do all the jobs in the business and grow it by dint of their unflagging effort and willingness to work long hours. Eventually, they earn an income that is three times what they could have made just by holding down a job.

Unfortunately, they are earning that income by doing the work of three people. That is my definition of a "Mom and Pop" company. The owner is making a living, but ironically the only way to improve that living is by further denigrating his or her lifestyle.

A local distribution business may have $10,000,000 in revenue, but operates with a half dozen employees and the owners. Their profit before taxes could be as little as $200,000 – putting this $10 million business squarely in the category of "Mom and Pop."

Mom and Pop business owners are seldom candidates for exit planning. When they stop working, the business ceases to exist. Their best hope is usually to pass it to a family member or employee who is also willing to work really hard to earn a decent living. There is seldom enough free cash flow to support much in the way of debt for the purchase of the company.

Middle-Market Businesses

Middle-Market businesses are defined by investment bankers as having revenues between $100 million and $3 billion with less than 2,000 employees. The US Department of Commerce lists the parameters as between $10 million and $250 million in revenue. One accounting association says the "lower middle market" is classified as companies between $5 million and $100 million. Investopedia.com pegs it as $10 million to $1 billion. Divestopedia.com goes with $5 million to $500 million. TheStreet.com has the widest range at $5 million to $1 billion.

Of course, a $5 million revenue company could easily have much less than $500,000 in pre-tax earnings, which would put it squarely in the Main Street category. On the other hand, a substantial number of software and Internet-based companies have become "unicorns" (over $1 billion in market valuation) with far less than $100 million in revenue.

This discussion is only intended to make two points. First, few people know exactly what they are referring to when they say "Main Street" or "Middle-Market." They have their own idea and definition, which is fine. Unfortunately, it is unlikely that the person they are talking to has the same definition.

Second, advisors who say they "don't work with Main Street" are probably uninformed. Many Main Street business owners are excellent candidates for exit planning. In fact, according to the 2022 National Exit Planners Survey™ – exitplannerssurvey.com, when the $3,000,000 fair market value yardstick is specified, two-thirds of exit planning professionals say that 50% or more of their clients are in that category.

If you enjoy musings like this, please subscribe to my blog at Awakeat2oclock.com or to the "Rifle" mailing list (it's a long story) by emailing rifle@exitmap.com.

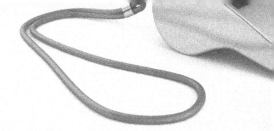

SOURCES:

1. Exit Planning Institute 2013 State of Owner Readiness Survey, 2021 PriceWaterhouseCoopers, Whose Business Is It Anyway? Smart Strategies for Ownership Succession, and University of Connecticut Family Business Program, Family Business Survey
2. U.S. Small Business Administration and US Census Bureau
3. 2022 National Exit Planners Survey
4. Brookings Institution, Occupational Licensing – a Framework for Policy Makers – White House report - July 2015
5. US Social Security Administration
6. Cornell- SC Johnson College of Business
7. PriceWaterhouseCoopers Survey of Business Owners 2018
8. US Census Bureau
9. US Small Business Administration
10. Pepperdine Capital Markets Survey and International Business Brokers Association (multiple years)
11. The Economist
12. US Small Business Administration
13. US Bureau of Labor Statistics (Investopedia)
14. Pepperdine Capital Markets Survey and International Business Brokers Association (multiple years)
15. Cornell- SC Johnson College of Business